THE RHYME

OF THE

LADY OF THE ROCK

AND HOW IT GREW

BY

EMILY PFEIFFER

"All the strength, and all the arts of men, are measured by,
and founded upon, their reverence for the passion, and their
guardianship of the purity, of Love."

RUSKIN

LONDON

KEGAN PAUL, TRENCH, & CO., 1 PATERNOSTER SQUARE

1884

Envoy

TO

C. R. AND M. L.

Sweet sisters, far away in space, but near
    In love, to you this shapen thought I bring
    As 'twere a jewel that might clasp or cling,
Well knowing that however it appear
To others poor, your loves will hold it dear ;
    And all the dearer that the song I sing
    Is mine, and verily the only thing
That I can truly give of all my gear.

Sisters ! None better than we three can know
    Where absence tells on love, where tries in vain ;
The hearts it cannot quell it worketh woe ;
    And thus I send o'er land and sea, this chain
To bind your thoughts to me an hour or so
    In links that shall be other than of pain.

THE RHYME

OF THE

LADY OF THE ROCK.

—o—

In the autumn of the year 18—, we were tarrying
at Oban, detained against our will by the storm
which caused the great Atlantic waves, despite the
natural breakwater of Kerrera, and the many protect-
ing headlands of the bay, to come surging almost
into the houses of the overgrown Highland village.
Looking, from the blurred windows of the Great
Western Hotel, upon the wild waste of sea which sub-
merged the garden, we might almost have fancied ourselves where about this time we had counted upon
being : on the often turbid waters at the mouth of
Loch Linnhe, on our passage to the Island of Mull.
We were fain to acknowledge, in hearing of the
wind and the waves, that we were in a better place,
as, admiring the play of the mighty forces from our
safe shelter, we abided our time.

A

It was, perhaps, on the day following the storm,
when the shingle, which had turned the high road
into a pebbly beach, had been cleared away, when
the clean, porous soil of the Western Highlands
had left the surface dry, and the sun had made a
rift in the retiring storm-clouds, that we ventured
abroad, hoping to obtain from Dunolly a glimpse of
Castle Duart, the old Norse-built stronghold which
formerly made terrible to strangers the entrance to
the Sound of Mull, having been long the headquarters of chiefs who exercised a wild sovereignty
over the Isles.

Duart Castle, and the low, black, almost sunken
rock which lies betwixt it and Lismore Lighthouse,
had ever since I first beheld them, on a summer
holiday long years ago, possessed a peculiar interest
for me, as having been the scenes of a highly dramatic
story, the yet unexhausted capacity of which for
poetic treatment, had lately been pointed out to me
by my friend Professor Blackie. It was at his in-
stigation that I had also got hold of a little-known
book by one calling himself a "senachie" of the
Clan Maclean, which in its turn introduced me to
other curious sources of information; and these
several circumstances abetting, my mind had come
to set with considerable persistency in the direction
of this old robbers' nest, and was busying itself by

night and by day with recalling the life of a time in
which, notwithstanding that it was some few years
in advance of the battle of Flodden, the annals of
this part of Scotland were as wild and bloody as
they could have been in the earliest dawn of civilisation.

To our sore disappointment we found on arriving
at Dunolly gate that this was a day on which no
visitors were admitted to the grounds ; and we retired
after a short parley, with a peculiar sense of injury,
owing to the enclosure to which we were debarred
entrance being a bit of the coast, which I suppose
presents itself to the natural imagination as a sort
of "no man's land," of which it is presumptuous for
any individual to claim exclusive possession. Somewhat sulkily turning our steps inland, we gradually
recovered our equanimity in mounting the hill, as a
pause or two and a backward look showed us the
lovely bay broadening itself to the view and allowing
us a sight of the several outlets between the islands
which hem it in.

We had but just cleared the hill, had passed the
green " braes " to the left, and were proceeding, still
bent on obtaining if possible a glimpse of Castle
Duart, when we saw striding towards us from behind,
he also having mounted the hill on his way from the
town, a tall, elderly, but not old man, whose steady

gait and upright bearing betrayed the training of the
soldier. He held an umbrella by the ferule over his
shoulder, and depending from the crook of the handle
was a bundle tied in a cotton handkerchief. A pair
of kindly hospitable blue eyes had beamed a manner
of Highland welcome on the strangers as he drew
near, and I felt emboldened by their brightness to
ask if a view of the object of my persistent thoughts
was to be arrived at by a walk of a mile or two in
any direction from where we stood.

The wayfarer rose to the conception on the instant.
An English rustic would perhaps in his dull way have
thought scorn of us for the unprofitable contemplation,
but to our tall Highlander it appeared the most natural
thing in the world that people should go out of their
way to look at the distant silhouette of Castle Duart ;
and although, judging from his appearance, he would
himself have been as ready to walk twenty miles as
two, he at once gave to my narrow limitation the
easy acceptance of that good breeding which seems
native to the Celt. Castle Duart he told us might
be descried from the coast to which we had thought
of wending our way, but better and nearer at hand
could be sighted from a hill which he pointed out
at a short distance ahead of us, and to the summit
of which, if we would give him time to deposit his
bundle at his own cottage by the way, he would

willingly be our guide. In a minute he had caught up our sauntering steps. " Did he personally know anything of the Island of Mull?" The hospitable eyes gave out a little spark of blue fire. Did he know Mull? Well, yes, he was a Mull man, and he thought if being born and bred in a place, and his father, and father's fathers in all their generations having been born and bred in it, could help something towards the knowledge of the same, he might say he knew it very well. It was a beautiful island —the Island of Mull; there was nothing between you and the New World when you looked out over the ocean from the far side of it. Most any seed would grow there that you put into the ground, but it was little that the soil of Mull was given to work upon in these latter days; the land went all out of cultivation. Where a score of families, with a due proportion of strong men among them, might have lived and thriven, you'd often enough find only a skeleton of an old woman, who had chosen rather to haunt the graves where the most of her kin lay buried, than to emigrate with the remnant that the wars had spared to her youth, and the famine to her old age.

While we were thus talking we had begun slowly to ascend the hill, off the road to the right, yet not so slowly but that after a time I had to halt

and refresh myself with a quiet look at the world
which, at the height from which we gazed, was
getting to show itself round.   The eyes of our Highland friend, who was acquainted with every detail of
the scene, seemed to rest upon it with a satisfaction
from which familiarity had taken nothing of the gusto.

While we thus stood, one of us, I, or my companion, asked him wherefore he had chosen to settle
on the mainland rather than in the island which was
the home of his race.   As no immediate answer
came to this question, I glanced up and saw that
the features of the Islesman were rigidly set, his
colour considerably heightened : he was evidently
struggling with some emotion that he was determined
to keep in check.   The absence of self-consciousness,
and his simple good faith, soon gave him the desired
advantage, and we had the rare pleasure of listening
for a while to talk which was no echo of a foregone
state of feeling or perception, but vital and aglow
with emotional forces that were then and there in
operation.   This was happening early in September,
with only a month between us and the last vapid
dregs of the London season ; and the living words
with their slow, sustained vibration seemed to help,
with the breezy hill-side, the storm-clouds sweeping the sky, and the rounding world, to freshen our
jaded spirits.   Our guide had now raised his head,

and as he spoke, looked intently into each of our faces by turn.

"You wish to know why I chose to settle down here, in lieu of returning to Mull? I did not choose, I was driven to it. I left Mull in my twentieth year, to join my regiment, for I had 'listed for a soldier. I served in the Crimea; I was at Inkerman, and the taking of the Redan, and Sebastopol itself. After a while, we were ordered for India. No one that has so much as heard of it will ever forget the Mutiny, no one that has lived through it will ever get the sights out of their eyes, nor the sounds out of their ears; war, man against man, is bad enough, but that was a war with devils. Well, I served through it with the rest. I was afterwards in Afghanistan. I was afterwards in China. We had a warm time of it, marching and fighting, fighting and marching; most of us were grey before we had gone far. Many a day when the sun hung a dull red ball in the sky as if it had burnt itself out, and the jungle was all bars and stripes, black and yellow like a tiger's skin, and we tramping along 'neath our heavy trappings, raising the dust as we went, have I counted the days to the distant time when I should be brushing my feet through the dewy bell heather in the Island of Mull—for there is a deal of soft weather in Mull, lady, more it's likely than may seem good to strangers com-

ing from south of the Tweed—but the remembrance
of it would rush upon me now and again in that
Indian heat, and in a manner freshen me to bear it.
Our time of service was wearing away ; many, most
of the old faces were gone, and those that remained
were set more and more towards home.   My day of
release came at last ; I had earned my pension ; I
was a free man, with my little hoard of money, and
my good character,—for not in all the lengthened
time I had served, had ever a mark been set against
my name in the regimental books, and I carried with
me the certificate of the same, ready to show to any
one it might concern.

"We landed at Portsmouth ; before night I was off
north ; the following day I was at home in Mull.
My father was dead, my sisters were married and
away, but the bit cottage and garden were there, just
as I remembered them, and the cottage stood empty,
as it might be waiting my return.   I was glad of my
pension then, and more than all of the money I had
saved from drink.

"The estate had passed into other hands, but I
learned where the new gentleman was to be found, and
lost no time in getting to see him.   He was a very
pleasant-speaking gentleman.   I showed him my
papers,—my certificate of service, and the rest ; and
told him I should dearly like to buy the old place if

I could pay his price, or to rent it of him if he was not minded to sell it. He said something about my having been tried in the fire and come out sound; he was a very civil spoken gentleman, and told me to go next day in the morning to his factor, the man who managed all the business of the estate, and doubted not he'd put the matter straight for me.

"I did go to the factor next day, though backwards and forwards, between his house—a beautiful house—and two or three out-lying farms, it was well-nigh evening before I came to speech of him. Well, I stated my wishes, and the hopes his chief had led me to entertain, and was coming out with my papers, when he put me back with his hand, and began walking by the side of me towards the open door.

"'It's no manner of use, my man,'—I mind his words,—'it's no manner of use going further into this; you're not the sort of tenant that's wanted on the estate, and we don't mean to sell at no price; so you'd best go quiet about your business, for no noise won't help you.' I asked him if he'd be good enough to signify what were the conditions I failed in; but he'd backed me over the threshold by this, and without another word had clapped the door in my face. I stood a minute or two in the rain, looking right and left; and then I went back by the road I had come. I lingered about the village for more than a week, trying in many

ways to get speech again of the gentleman ; but he
denied himself when I called, and made off when he
saw me in the distance ; there was nothing to be
hoped from him any more than from his steward."

The muscles of the veteran's nether jaw had again
become tense, but his sensitive, strongly featured face
was now set straight towards us in its indignant
sorrow, and frank appeal for sympathy.   There was
something positively thrilling in the low deliberate
voice as it passed over the tightened chords :

"I had spent eight and twenty years, tossed about
by land and sea, in active service for my Queen and
country ; had I returned to Mull from having worked
out my time in a penal settlement, the welcome I
found there could have been no rougher than it was."

We felt the pathos of this simple eloquence, and
did not care to inquire closely into the case which
the "honourable men," the strangers in Mull, who
made life impossible to the sons of the soil, could
doubtless have made out for themselves.   As we stood
face to face with the old soldier in the spangled
heather which he had seen in many a mirage of the
mind, suddenly brought together upon ground that
was purely human, our little party of three was en-
tirely at one.   It took us some minutes of time, and
a good deal of vigorous expression of feeling, to get
the moral atmosphere about us calm and clear ; and

before this was effected, we were once more following
our guide in his zigzag path, over the shoulder of the
hill, I steadied as occasion required by his helpful
hand, and kept dry-shod to the end by his intimate
knowledge of every firmer tussock of grass upon
which a foot could be planted. During another short
halt he continued :

" It felt bad to be crossing the Sound of Mull with
Castle Duart at the back and Dunolly to the fore ;
but there was neither work nor welcome in the old
place, and I was as mad to get out of it as I had
been fain to get in. A ball shot from a cannon
might feel like that ; I was going,—the farther the
better. When I landed at Oban pier, I came along
here, not knowing or caring much where I should
stop. I turned off the high road where we turned
awhile agone, and I came up here, as we may be
coming now, and I saw—there, lady, stand upon
this stone, and you get the best view of it—I saw
just what you are looking at at this moment : the
Island of Mull with Duart Castle in front, and the
Lady's Rock, where a Maclean of Duart exposed
his wife in a high tide when a storm was on, a little
this side of it, and the Hills o' the Two Winds—Dun-
da-Ghaodh they call it in the Gaelic—and Craigienure, to the right from where we see it, and Loch
Don, and Loch Spelve to the left, and there, on the

other side of that tongue of land, Loch Buy, with
Moy Castle,—you may just catch it and Moy House
beyont the trees—and over all, when the weather is
fair and the wind in the west as it happed that day,
Ben Môr. It is a very fine view; so I got the
cottage where you saw me leave the bundle, and
morning or evening, or morning and evening as the
case may be, I come up most days to see it."

I looked with my naked eyes; I looked with the
field-glass that my companion adjusted for me; I
made out Castle Duart, and, guided by Lismore
Lighthouse, I made out the rock where the unhappy
lady, a sister of the third Earl of Argyle, had
awaited the onslaught of the waves; but withal I
failed to see the half of what was so apparent to the
eyes enlightened by early recollection. The gaze of
the banished man whose memory conjured up these
well-known pictures, seemed to travel from point to
point, pleased, with the pathetic acquiescence of the
Celt, that the mountains and woody or rocky headlands of his island home still held their wonted
place in the scheme of things. Here, then, at last
before me was the spot towards which my thoughts
had for a while been tending; but my pleasant anticipations concerning it, my new hopes, took on something of the sadness of the old regret of which I
stood within the shadow.

The day but one from this, we were steaming towards the Sound of Mull, our backs turned to
Dunolly, and our faces to Duart. The sea was
sufficiently quiet after its late disturbance, as we
passed Kerrera on the left and the Garden Isle on
the right ; came almost within hailing distance of
the Lady's Rock, and could note the very spot, the
highest ledge of it, which must have been the last
resort of the Lady Elizabeth when the rest of the
narrow reef was engulfed by the waves. Much as
we now saw it, frowning grimly from its rocky plat-
form, must have looked Castle Duart to the eyes of
the unhappy, and surely unwilling bride of the savage
and—rare distinction in a Highland chief—cowardly
Lachlan Maclean. Cut off from the mainland by the
treacherous gulf open to the stormy inroads of the
Atlantic, this daughter of the Campbells, as she gazed
for the first time upon those fourteen feet thick walls
of the Norse-built tower, was likely to have thought
with a strange sinking of the heart of the war-cry of
her clan, "'Tis a far cry to Loch Awe."

For our own part we were for the moment concerned
with a little farmhouse which lay within the shadow of
the inhospitable-looking pile ; since it was there that
we had made arrangements to take up our quarters
so long as we should remain in Mull. We could not
fail to be struck with the more than modest promise

of entertainment which the cottage offered, but its immediate vicinity to Duart, and the wild loneliness of its situation on its treeless tongue, or "nose," of land, commended it to us, and we passed on our way rejoicing; albeit a mist soon closed over the object of our regard, and the rain began to descend as we neared Craigienure. A little group of persons, and a quantity of various luggage, was crowding about the steamer's side by this time; all that had eyes were regarding with eager interest the progress of the boat which, rowed by a man and a boy, was nearing us from Craigienure jetty. In a minute every tongue of the whole group was in simultaneous action, question and answer being bandied between boat and steamer with a heartiness and a clannish indifference to outsiders which made us also realise that it was a "far cry" from this Island of Mull to the place and the people to whom we were of any account.

The boat came shoving alongside; every right hand in the excited little crowd was given to be grasped by the man and touched by the boy; the questions continued to pour down; little note was taken of the rain though it was beginning to do the same; cloaks were spread upon the damp seats, ladies and children were handed to their places; the variously featured luggage was hauled on board; a

party of children frantically left the hold of their elders
to see after some parcel containing toys.

"Where's the young laird whatever?"

"He's here."

"Hand him over."

"Can ye no mak' place for a chentleman and
leddy?" This from the steamer.

"As much as ever."

"Try then." The thing was tried, and succeeded;
we were wedged in among the others,—accounted, I
fear, as matter in the wrong place,—and the boat was
just about pushing off when a cry arose for a green
parrot, the most agonised being that of a lady known
to all present as Miss Maclean.

"In the lady's cabin."

"No, I brought it out myself."

"By the gangway."

"Carried aft."

"Under the rocking-horse."

"Can auld acquaintance be forgot?" croaked an
unearthly voice; and the green parrot was lowered
over the ship's side, and received into the boat with
acclamation. We pushed off; we landed at the
jetty; our little impedimenta were reclaimed with
difficulty from the mass, and we made our way under
our umbrellas to the inn. The lady and parrot had
just been tucked up in a pony-carriage, after profuse

greetings, and with passionate farewells were about
being driven off in one direction, while a waggonette
and dog-cart stood ready to bear the modern repre-
sentatives of the Clan Maclean on their sixteen-mile
journey in the other.   The children and servants
had swarmed into the inn, and the former were overflowing kitchen, parlour, and passages in a moment,
while the lady was increasing the store of local information gathered by the way, in a parley with the
hostess, whose soft voice might be heard between
whiles adjuring the maid-servant to hasten the boiling
of the kettle, and begging the laird's wife to take a
warm by the sitting-room fire.

As we stood before the door, observing all this in
the fine, soft, straight-falling rain, one of the little
girls of the chieftain's family rushed out to us, carrying what seemed in her familiar grasp like a big doll,
but which proved itself by its complaisant smiles to
be a baby, with an apparently hereditary fealty to
everything calling itself Maclean.   The manner in
which this infant suffered itself to be whisked about
and changed from one little weak arm to another of
this eight-year-old child, might have furnished a text
to a " scientist " like Mr. Galton.

" This is my god-child," said the little girl, un-
covering the young creature in the rain, and tossing
it about under the horses' heads in a manner which

seemed to imply that the relationship had given her power of life and death over it.

The Maclean, or Loch Buy as we heard him called, a stalwart, sandy-bearded, ruddy-fleshed Highlander, was looking to his cattle preparatory to their wet return-journey over deep and hilly roads; and the whole party and their belongings were in due time packed into the vehicles and whirled away, especial reverence being shown to the person of the little laird, who, folded in a plaid, was placed next his father on the box.

When the Loch Buy party in the first carriage, and their following to the last band-box in the second, were finally lost to sight in a turn of the road, our own inferior claims became the subject of regard.

The host of the inn at Craigienure (Gaelic : The Point of Look-out) turned upon us a face full of the ready sympathy of a race which, ancient as it is, still possesses the grace of youth. A tall, brown, well-shaped man, his movements and speech had something of the distinction which comes from an air of abundant leisure. Host though he was, he laid no fussy embargo upon our persons, but looked at us as one who was ready, if need were, to do us service. In answer to our expectation that some conveyance might have been sent for us from the farm, he informed us with minute knowledge of the

B

circumstance, that Archie Cumming's old horse
Smiler was at the moment lame in the off fore-leg,
and added, that barring that accident the lady, if she
had been used to springs, might not have fancied the
rough ride in the Cumming's trap. The non-appear-
ance of anything in the shape of rolling-stock from
Duart was accounted for, and it was needless to
admit the impeachment of effeminate prejudice : so
we limited ourselves to a request to be conveyed to
our destination by such means as Craigienure could
supply.

Craigienure could do nothing for us ; its one horse
was far a-field in a direction pointed out, carrying a
neighbour's hay (a damp load it must have been by
this time), and it was uncertain when it might return.
The awkwardness of our situation was apparent.
We moved towards the open door, at which the
landlady, with a face of kind concern, had been
listening to the colloquy. With the baby in her
arms, and a lovely little girl at her side, she made
room for us to enter, and at once, with the help of
her ruddy-armed maid, busied herself for our entertainment. She herself was a soft, much expanded,
large-eyed creature, not young for a nursing mother,
but with a look which she had in common with her
surroundings, rather of dilapidation than of age.
The little up-stair parlour had a welcome aspect ;

there were pots of growing flowers in the two windows, one at either end, and a brisk fire in the grate. A short council was held, and that one of us who takes for his share all the worst of the work of life, determined to set out in the rain for the three-and-a-half-mile walk to Duart, and, "the lady's" use of springed vehicles having hitherto been too exclusive to afford her any measure of the inconvenience resulting from their absence, to see if the present condition of Smiler might admit of his being used in our service, or failing that, to gather from personal observation what means the farm had to offer as a place of sojourn if ever we might attain to it.

The rain from a drizzle became a down-pour; the strange road with its several turns, and the varied obstacles to progress presented by the trees which had been felled by the storm, and by the wind and the sheeted rain, both striving, as it seemed, to bar the way upon the shelterless waste, appeared interminable to the pedestrian, and the Farm Cottage which was gained at length looked but a frail haven against such inhospitable forces. Not so, however, thought its inmates, who, at sight of the strugglingly advancing umbrella, had gathered to the door in a flutter of joyous excitement. The half-breathless wayfarer was drawn within, divested of his dripping overcoat, hurried to a warm corner by the hearth, plied in turn, and I

fear in vain, with every species of refreshment from
hot drinks to cold bacon, and eagerly questioned as
to what had been done for the nonce with the lady
whose appearance was still confidently looked forward
to. The good people were reluctantly made to understand that they must yield up their present guest again
to the rough dealing of the weather; and nothing short
of the delightful prospects of the near future and the
endless hospitable preparations which could still be
made for it, seemed capable of supporting Archie
Cumming's aunt and housekeeper under the trial of
letting the stranger forth. Withal, he was by no
means to be suffered to return as he had come, but
Smiler must be put to, and one or more little arrangements made with the trap and harness, to get it in
working order. A delicate inquiry as to Smiler's
health was met by the assurance that his lame leg
was practically the best of four, all good; while the
trap, which was under hasty repair, and which was
known as "the machine," was spoken of with the
solemnity befitting an instrument supposed to confer
some social distinction on its possessors.

In point of fact the difficulties of the encumbered
road were much aggravated to a good walker by the
pomp and circumstance of the return journey, and the
day was well on before the traveller reached Craigienure.
From the wary way in which Smiler had put his off fore-

leg to the ground, it was clear that he did not labour under the same delusion in regard to it as his owner; and the "milk of human kindness" which had flowed responsive to that which had met him so abundant at the farm, was perhaps a trifle curdled in the traveller's breast by the severe churning of the "machine." A collie, accustomed from his position to make the best of chance companionship and altogether to draw the sweets from the passing moment, wagged his tail at him on his return to the Craigienure Arms; the lovely little maid of the inn peered at him from out a shadowy passage, which she brightened with her eyes and golden hair; the landlady greeted him with her pathetic smile; the landlord's voice was cheery; the room above was bright with flowers and glowing with the merry flame of a good coal fire; the same welcome light came dancing out of the half-open door of the neighbouring bed-chamber; the table was covered with a white cloth and other preparations for dinner, and the savour of a leg of delicate Highland mutton made itself distinctly felt above the sweet-williams. The sum-total of argument was irresistible. The Farm Cottage, frowned upon by that vicious old Castle, alone under its shadow upon the dreary waste, wind-swept, and storm-beaten, howled at and threat-ened by land and sea, painted itself in undesirable colours upon the mind of the weather-beaten traveller;

and the impossibility of getting away from it when once there, of exploring the neighbourhood with any assistance to your own powers of locomotion, determined us to abandon the idea of taking Duart as our headquarters, when all that was wanted might be got out of it by an occasional visit.

The mutton was found to keep its promise, the beds were clean, the entertainers kindly. A note was despatched to Duart Farm, in which much stress was laid upon our erratic intentions; and, not to commit Smiler in the incontinent revelation of his sad secret, Craigienure was alleged to be preferable to Duart in point of situation, as a starting-place for frequent and long expeditions.

Did I say that this note was despatched? Not so; the note was written, and left our hands, with a sum enclosed which we hoped would indemnify the good people at the farm for any inconvenience involved in our change of plan. But if the despatch of a letter be held to imply its delivery, the affair is not so hurriedly achieved in the Island of Mull.

When on the following day we found our way to Duart in the Craigienure dog-cart, Archie Cumming's aunt rushed, beaming like the sun which was also radiant overhead, to greet us, and almost took away our breath, quite impeded our hesitating utterance, with the torrent of acts and words which went to her

Highland welcome. A beautiful little Maltese spaniel, with an air too daintily civilised for her surroundings, was also penetrated with her mistress's spirit, and adopted us on the instant, manifesting her goodwill in a series of joyous yelps and graceful gambols which seemed rather to belong to the renewal than the commencement of acquaintance. It became immediately evident that no note had been received, and that the pleasing anticipations of human society and service which had been active in this kindly soul from the moment she had agreed to our sojourn under her roof, had resulted in such an overflow during the night as made the task of undeceiving her, with which we were now brought face to face, a matter of very appreciable pain.

"Will you have something to eat after your drive, or a mouthful of milk and whisky, or take a warm by the fire first before putting off your things? You'll ha' been long on the road, for the ruts is deep after the rain, and they tell me the half o' the trees in the wood you'll ha' come by is laid by the storm; it will ha' been a rough ride in the Craigienure trap; will you rest awhile, or will I show you to your room, and after that you can "——

"You do not know, Miss Macorquodale,—you have not received the letter?"

"The letter? no; what for should you write whatever? It will happen be something you are wanting that we haven't got; but I can go myself to Oban; oh, I can get to Craigienure before the steamer touches there the morn, and I can be back again here by nightfall; and anything that is to be had in the world can be got at Oban, and I shall find it for you, and bring it with me before you can feel the want of it."

The piece of work before us was becoming harder with every moment of delay. The bearer of burthens gave a hand to it here.

"I wrote to tell you, Miss Macorquodale," he said, "that we have made up our minds to remain at Craigienure, finding it a better starting-place for the excursions we are to make by land and sea. We are very sorry to give up Duart, and I am afraid you may be disappointed too, but—in short, you will see by the letter;—the letter will tell you "—— Yes, what we could not; how we mentally adjured its aid!

A great change had come over the hospitable face and attitude of Miss Macorquodale; the spirit that had appeared to greet us at eyes and lips had now turned within, and shut to the door upon her injured feelings; she sank into a chair, she was visibly paler; I think she even trembled a little, and was glad of some support.

"We are very, very sorry," I echoed helplessly; "I

know we could have made ourselves so happy here."
Impossible to tell the stately personage who had
suddenly raised such a barrier between us in her
struggle to appear unperturbed, what the letter had
offered of simple justice; and we sat before her
condemned without power of appeal.

"You have made such preparation for us," I said,
unconsciously aggravating our case. " I am afraid
you have had no end of trouble."

"Dhu not think of it," returned Miss Macorquodale with crushing magnanimity; "just a journey
to Oban for myself to collect the things that are not
grown upon the farm, and a few days' work for the
'girls' to set all straight; and the chickens that we
killed on Wednesday, and the butter that I churned
the day, and the baking of white bread, and the
scones, and the baps; dhu not think about it,—it
is nothing."

" But indeed it is a great deal ;—if—if only Duart
had been a little less out of the way."

" It iss a fery convenient place," affirmed Miss
Macorquodale, " but it iss not good enough for you.
The inn at Craigienure will be noisy, but you will
happen have been used to noise. You cannot keep
a house of business clean with poor health, and only
one girl, and a hantle of bairns, but no more can you
the fine houses in the big towns for the dust and

smoke. You will accept a pound of the Duart butter
that iss not to be had in any market for being all
bespoke before made by the gentry far and near.
It iss the butter that can tell !"

Miss Macorquodale, somewhat relieved by her own
eloquence, rose as she spoke, and opening wide a
cupboard, scrubbed and orderly to its farthest corner,
she produced a dish of her own butter, and flanking
it with the newly baked bread and a plate of scones,
she suffered it awhile to bear silent testimony, while
she sat stiffly regarding it with pardonable pride. Miss
Macorquodale was right : there is probably no witness
to the housewifely virtues so conclusive as butter.
Perceptions blunted by the no more than conditional
cleanliness possible to great towns may be slow to
detect deficiency ; but the butter everywhere can tell.
We remained for a second or two in admiring contemplation. The colour of Miss Macorquodale's
butter was clear and rich, its elements perfectly
united, its substance apparently consistent in just
the right degree ; it was cunningly made up, and
daintily set forth ; we could not help contrasting it
with the far less meritorious product supplied to the
inn breakfast-table. I fondly hoped that our un-
stinting praise of the seemingly perfect emollient
might have a softening effect, but Miss Macorquodale
evidently understood her advantage, and was not

minded lightly to forego it. We were offenders, and
although she was too proud to complain of injury, she
was not above punishing transgression.

While she had been engaged in furnishing her table,
I had time to take note of her person and its adornments. She was long past middle age, stout and
active, with a face which had in it neither beauty nor
ugliness to take from the single impression of goodness;
a pair of lively eyes, a short nose, a long upper lip;
a homely face, a mask, but a very transparent one,
telling you as distinctly of something behind it that was
worth the quest, as many a beautiful face will tell you
that the best it has to show has been already seen.
A jacket of scarlet cloth overlapped petticoats of convenient length, meaning that they were a good seven
inches clear of the soles of her stout shoes. So far
the outward woman might have composed well in a
picture taken of Duart Castle and Farm; but a dull
consistency is not a common attribute of actual life,
and my obligation to truth compels me to confess
that the picturesque scarlet jacket and grey locks of
Miss Macorquodale were surmounted by a cap in which
the effigy of a pink rose was a conspicuous object.
The artist who works with words has this advantage
over the painter who relies upon pigments : he comes
into more direct contact with the soul of his subject.
Thus the singular toilet arrangements of Mr. Cum-

ming's aunt which would have made a false note upon canvas, may easily be shown when verbally dealt with, to have added a little touch not far from pathetic to her otherwise ordinary exterior.   The incongruous head-gear clearly represented an effort to meet our supposed supra-mundane tastes, and the very abortiveness of this attempt to commend her homely person, touched a deeper underlying chord of human sympathy.   Looking at Miss Macorquodale and reading her by the indications offered, I became more than ever anxious to propitiate her favour.

"There are many places in Mull that can best be got at by sea," I said, returning to the one plea which I felt to be void of offence, "and the steamer you know does not touch here, but at Craigienure."

"There iss the machine," returned Miss Macorquodale ; "it takes me every Sabbath to the kirk, and it iss no harder to get to the boat.   But do not be sorry whatever ; it iss no matter ; Duart is fery convenient and easy for all things, and it iss healthy and beautiful air, but it iss not good enough for you."

"It is as good and better than anything we are likely to get," I rejoined.   Do not let it be supposed that my desire to improve my position with Miss Macorquodale led me to untruthful concession, since the aspect of Duart was very different seen as now under the soft sunshine, and as it had been beheld yesterday, blown upon and blurred by wind and rain.

" I like it better than Craigienure," I insisted ; " I love the quiet,—and then the view ! "

` " The view is the finest in the Western Highlands," averred Miss Macorquodale with an air of studied dis- interestedness ; " but you will have been used to the carriages, and the fine houses and streets which they tell me are as light by night as they are by day, and it iss only mountains we have got to show, and the Sound of Mull, and the ruined castles, and nothing but the stars at night, and now and then the "——— Was the pitiless old woman about to add the moon, or the Aurora ? I cannot say, for I broke in upon her at this point, feeling that she was capable of twitting me with the corona of the sun.

" I do not live in a street," I pleaded, " and I hate noise and gas, and look upon smoke as one of the deadly sins."   I was really anxious to free my surroundings from a suspicion of vulgarity which provoked a scorn wearing so fine a veil. " I love the mountains," I continued, " and the sweet air, and the silence, and more than all, the sea ; and I like Duart Farm, and I like your butter, Miss Macorquodale, and your little dog, and I should like to like you if you would let me."

Miss Macorquodale persisted in looking past me, but I saw signs of relenting in the corners of her mouth. He who should have stood by me in this struggle had for once thrown down his arms, and fled from a contest in which patience and nimbleness were of more account than strength.

There had been moments when my eye had swept the long perspective of the road visible through the window, ready to hail a man with a letter-bag as a deliverer ; but now a change had taken place in my feelings. I could not have faced Miss Macorquodale with that packet in her hand which had so confidently been directed to her only last evening ; it was clearly the sentimental aspect of the injury done her that alone occupied her mind; and our attempt at money compensation now appeared to be a proceeding as gross as that of putting a price upon wounded affections. I saw with relief that a step which had startled me had been only that of an inquisitive donkey, the road as far as eye could reach being clear of the postman ; so with renewed courage, I returned to the charge.

" If I did not fear that you were too angry with me, I would still ask you a favour, Miss Macorquodale."

" An' it iss fery kind of you," she responded with Celtic readiness of intuition, " but it will be only that you think I am lonely, and should like to have heard your voices, and to wait upon you by day or by night, as it iss true ; you can see that, and you are sorry I am disappointed ; but it iss no matter ; I shall just work the harder with the girls for a day or two, and it will go over. The place iss a good place enough, but it iss not good enough for you."

"You are unforgiving, Miss Macorquodale, and you are hard upon me. I am sorry you are disappointed, but I am also disappointed myself. I want still to come to Duart, and I mean to persuade you now to take us in—yes, I do—in a week from this time, and if you are obstinate and refuse us the shelter of your roof, I shall go and lodge in that wicked-looking old tower that has none."

"No, dear, you shall come here, and you shall have the best of everything that the poor place can give you," cried Miss Macorquodale. "But the gentleman? What will the gentleman say? I think he has got a will of his own."

"I know he has; but his will in coming to Mull was to please me, and he doesn't do things by halves. When he first saw Duart, it was under a cloud; to-day it is different."

"Well, say nothing for sure till you ha' seen your room upstairs," conceded Miss Macorquodale, blooming and brightening until the rose in her cap seemed no longer an isolated spot; and with much inward rejoicing I followed the scarlet jacket as it led the way to the chamber above. The accommodation offered was undoubtedly primitive, and in spite of the orderli-

ness and purity of all that properly fell under the juris-
diction of Mr. Cumming's aunt, the Celtic feeling of
letting things go, was apparent in the state of the walls
and the roof, which at a tolerably safe distance from the
bed must occasionally have given ingress to the rain.
The one small window looked out upon the old Castle
and the green slope that led up to it, and beyond
that, to the graves of the soldiers who had died at
Duart when, in the last century, it had been a garrison.

The bed and the bedding, which was turned down
for my inspection, were found to be of delicate nicety,
and to the tremulous joy of Miss Macorquodale I
expressed myself more than content.

"The blankets have been spun by myself from the
wool of our own sheep," she said; "they are light
and warm, for there is no cotton in them; but I
have better, oh, I have better now that I have seen
you, but the best that I have it iss not good enough
for you!"

It was the fourth time that this formula had been
pronounced in my hearing within the last quarter of
an hour, but how different was the ring of this last
outburst to all that had gone before. The rich
nature of the woman, the nature at once impulsive
and leal, had asserted itself, and disappointment and
offence were alike forgotten in the flattering anticipations of human interchange. The barrier of wounded

pride had broken down, and she showed, as she proved herself to the last, so prompt to devotion as to be subject to generous illusion.

"Oh, but I am happy!" she exclaimed; "my heart warmed to you before ever you opened your mouth, when you sat up there in the Craigienure machine."

Now in beginning these introductory pages I had meant to report the truth, the whole truth, and nothing but the truth, but Miss Macorquodale's words in this place were so lamentably wide of the fact that I hold it better to suppress them. Since she was no vulgar flatterer, I am inclined to think—it being notorious that the Highland Scots have the gift of second sight—that what she saw in the Craigienure machine was my angel sitting in my place.

"It is a poor place for you to come to,—you'll ha' been used to the first of everything, and you don't look strong whatever; and maybe the machine will not seem easy to you, and Smiler iss not what he was; but the air it iss fine, and the fresh milk, and the cream; and all that there iss in the house or about the place iss yours for the willing, and I to serve you early and late." We were again in the parlour; the place found ready favour with my companion—a point upon which I had been sufficiently enlightened before venturing on my proposal. And here, as circumlocu-

C *

tions are always inconvenient, and designation by initial letters a hindrance to characterisation, let me assort to him who has been hitherto thus spoken of, the good Teutonic and suggestive name of Helmuth.

Miss Macorquodale had plunged into the dairy through the kitchen, leaving Helmuth and me to-gether to settle matters, and now returned bearing a pitcher of milk which it was evident she had slyly enriched with a liberal dash of cream. Having partaken of this refreshment as we felt bound, we were eager to be shown the Castle, and proceeded thither in company of our hostess, who was its custodian.

Judged in relation to Scottish strongholds gene-rally, Duart gives evidence of having been a place of considerable importance, not only from its com-manding position, crowning as it does a rock at the entrance of the Sound, but also for its size and the character of its accommodation, both unusual in the rude ages when chiefs of mighty clans allowed for little more light and space in their solidly built towers than is to be found in the habitations of beavers. From the side of Mull, which in early times was occupied wholly by Macleans, it would appear that no hostile attack was in a general way expected, for the door by which we entered after a slight ascent

from the farm, though stout and iron-clamped, had
no indication of having been further defended. It
gave ingress at once to a courtyard or quadrangle,
which was flanked on the left hand by one of the
mighty walls of the old tower, and on the right by
a pile of building containing in its basement what
seemed to have been offices, cellars, dungeons, and
the like. Opposite to the gate the quadrangle is
bounded by the great hall and the chambers above
it, all looking into the enclosure; while on the side
by which we had entered, it is shut in only by a high
wall. Beyond the great hall, raised a little above
its level, and looking sea-ward, is a large apartment,
presumably once the gathering place of the ladies of
the household, and the maidens whose labours they
directed; and my reading had apprised me that
among those who here wore out their lives many had
been princesses of the royal line of Scotland. The
entire pile is now roofless, and, with the exception
of the tower, impregnable by time as it has been by
other assault, in an advanced stage of decay. Martins
had built their nests in the crumbling stonework
which once frowned defiance upon passing ships;
chaffinches chattered from the little green sprays
which replaced the tapestries upon the walls; and of
all the present inmates of the once jealously guarded
fortress, the field-mouse alone was startled by our

invasion. We lingered awhile in the hall examining
its various features, and clomb the few remaining
steps of the turret stair which in one corner led from
it to the chambers above, and through one of them,
or a passage probably corresponding on each of two
floors, to subsidiary entrances to the upper rooms of
the tower. In that tower on the ground floor had
been the guard-room ; and the several posts of look-
out in the thickness of the wall, show how vigilant
a watch was there maintained. A winding stair,
broader and easier of ascent than that leading from
the hall, and hollowed like the posts of "look-out"
in the heavy masonry of the tower, leads from the
guard-room past the place once occupied by the two
chambers, of which the floors and ceilings have
given way, out upon the broad battlements beneath
the open sky.

And here from this vantage, turning our backs
on Mull, we obtained our first view of that scene
which Miss Macorquodale had been justified in an-
nouncing as the finest in the Western Highlands.
Straight ahead the eye sweeps past the silvery depths
of Loch Linnhe to the hills which rise in the direction of Bannavie and Fort William ; a little to the
right, over Loch Crearan, are the peaks of Glencoe ;
and soft in the distance, tender as the memory of the
absent or dead, rises the firm if faint outline of Ben

Cruachan, the rugged guardian of that peri of lakes, Loch Awe. Still further to the right appear the islands and peaks of Jura and of Colonsay, while on the left across the Sound of Mull stretch the Kingairloch, Morven, and Ardnamurchan hills.

As the day on which our first acquaintance with this lordly scene was made chanced to be especially clear, the ruins of almost all those castles which stood as sentinels on the islands and along the coast, were distinctly visible. First in order, to the right, rises Dunolly, the attitude of which in respect to Duart has passed into a proverbial expression of hostile relation; next a few crumbling walls behind Lismore Lighthouse indicate the position once occupied by the castle of Auchindown; Ardtornish, at the entrance to Loch Aline, is very noticeable; and Aros and Killundine, almost facing each other on either side the Sound, may be descried farther on. The remaining strongholds completing the system of defence which so jealously guarded the turbulent independence of the Lords of the Isles, though capable of communication by signals, were too faint and distant to make their presence felt by the unaided sense, from our point of observation.

Facing about, with our backs turned directly upon Loch Linnhe and all the soft splendours of sea and land which had unveiled themselves upon that side, our eyes wandered over a rather desolate view of

depopulated Mull.   Immediately below and about
us was the farm of Archie Cumming, poor-looking,
scarcely enclosed grazing-land, fields of turnips of
doubtful promise, and of oats slowly ripening to the
harvest.   Only on the side of the Sound, between
us and Craigienure, the broad, richly cultivated lands,
and umbrageous park and woods of Mr. Guthrie,
represented the happier results of which the island
under better conditions was capable.

Having made the round of the broad battlements,
and admired the amazing strength of their skilful
masonry, we descended the winding stair, and then
parted company, Helmuth going under the guidance
of Miss Macorquodale to inspect the live-stock, and
afterwards to seek and make acquaintance with our
future host.   I had pleaded to be left alone in the
castle for awhile, and found a seat on the deep stonework of a window in that apartment looking out upon
the sea, which I had fixed upon as likely to have
been assigned to the use of the ladies of Duart.   I
remained there dreaming very contentedly, listening
to the measured wash of the waves.   It was a spot
at once to soothe and to stimulate, to put everyday
thoughts to sleep, and to stir the memory and fancy.
I was losing by degrees the sense of the present;
the aggressions of time were made good, the walls
became clothed, the groined roof shut them in from

the blue vault above ; the hearth where the nettles were rampant was alive with the flames of resinous pines, given back from the bosses of shields, and shivering on the cruel spikes of spears ; for the armoury of this stronghold of the stormiest of the island lords had overflowed even into their ladies' bower. Shapes at first dim, but gathering consistency as the mind continued to give them entertainment, began to come and go before me, arranging themselves momently into scenes of the various dramas known to have been enacted in this lawless abode. My thoughts were at first tied to no time, but swept over the whole area of that family history with which I had been amusing my leisure.

The adventurous founder of the Clan Maclean is affiliated by tradition to the ancient kings of Ireland ; we may imagine what friction of stormy passions had made that country too hot to hold him, when he came, saw, and took possession of the moist island whose history has ever since been associated with his name. But the name itself was yet to make in those early days. MacGwillan was the form it first assumed, the accent falling on the final syllable, between which and the introductory Mac, the lazy habit of speech soon suppressed the soft fluid sounds which gave it its original music. To the foundation of the immovable tower which had presumably stood alone as the

lair of the earliest predatory chiefs, my information
did not enable me to go; and as the "Senachie"
already alluded to, writing of the clan in 1830, availing himself of all stores of knowledge within his
reach, and telling all, and perhaps more than all,
that he got to know, is silent on the subject, it may
be conjectured that nothing very certain about the
builder or the building of this ancient keep is recover-
able.   It was clear, however, that the court and the
surrounding pile which had been accreted to it,
though shaken and still crumbling, while the tower
stood whole and staunch, were the work of a later
period not difficult to define—a period when manners
even in this Ultima Thule had become humanised, and
when something of decency, and even of adornment,
had been added to life's barer need.   It was to a date
when no great advance had been made upon this
first movement of civilisation, slow everywhere, and
trebly slow in the Highlands of Scotland, that the
particular historical incident to which after awhile my
thoughts again gravitated, belonged.

    I was sitting, as has been said, on the window-
stone of what must have been the "lady's bower" of
those olden days, an apartment adjoining in its whole
length the great hall which looks out upon the quadrangle, as this upon the channel sea, and of that
history many of the chief scenes must have passed on,

or near to, this very spot.   The view obtainable from
this half-ruined window, of the lochs and islands with
their silvery background of mainland hills, was no
less lovely and little less extensive, than that which
we had seen from the summit of the tower; the sea
was dancing in the sun, which seemed to be casting
jewels into its shimmering surface; the shapes of the
objects far and near were clear as cameos, and soft
as film; but the changeful magic of beauty which
laid its spell upon the scene, forbade the mind coldly
to connote the details.

Calm as was the day, more breathlessly calm the
hour, there could be heard by one sitting alone in
the deserted chamber which had known the echoes of
so many generations of voices now passed into silence,
sounds as of sobbing, sighing, whispering, now here,
now there, but always in the direction of the sea.
The sounds breaking, and scarcely breaking, the
dreamy stillness, had a strangely furtive character,
ceasing apparently when questioned by the ear; and
coming again to mingle unbidden with the visions
which fancy had betaken itself to constructing.

That among the many exciting themes furnished
by the annals of this house my mind should recur
with a growing interest to the unhappy story of mari-
tal tyranny of which the reef called the Lady's Rock
was witness, is a circumstance that may be held to

explain itself. First, the rock was there, immediately
within sight, and might have invited the attention of
one less specially attracted by the story; and secondly,
a long course of reading having for its subject the
raids of a Highland clan in quest of plunder, and its
sanguinary struggles for supremacy, is in itself fitted
to produce upon the mind an impression so mono-
tonous in its savage violence, that an incident exhibit-
ing courage from its more human side, would naturally
appear as a relief. It was rest to turn from these
brutal struggles, that noise and confusion, to this
woman's silent suffering ; and it was joy to know her
to have been victorious.

Of a rare temper must have been the courage of
that lady, who having lived through the ordeal to
which a cunning malignity had exposed her, threat-
ened during hours of darkness by the fierce advance
and insufferable roar of the waves, and who, rescued
in the early dawn by one of the assistants in the
crime, and carried by him on the long and difficult
journey to her brother's castle, was able there, sane
in body as in mind, to take her part in that final scene
of the drama which reads like a page of old romance.

I began to gather up in my mind all the various
threads of the strange narrative, and fell insensibly
to weaving them into a connected whole. That
which art had already accomplished in this direction

I knew but very indistinctly, and had consciously refrained from inquiring into. The " Family Legend " of Joanna Baillie I had never read, and if I had at that time seen Campbell's ballad, it was among the many things which had left no trace in memory. I preferred going to the source to which in their turn these artists had doubtless gone, and dealing with the original material for myself. Thus I pondered over, till, as it seemed to me, I succeeded in penetrating by sympathy the motives which history in recording the outward act had left to be divined. What was everywhere firm under foot, too solid to admit of a doubt, was the general groundwork of character. In the case of Lachlan Cattenach Maclean the testimony is direct, and coming to us from many sources, meets always in one final conclusion : The man was a tyrant and a poltroon. But of the lady who was the subject of his lawless vengeance, the pity inspired by her sorrows seems to have confused the estimate. It is not unnatural that attempts should have been made to heighten the situation by representing the victim as soft and wholly unoffending, if not feeble and spiritless. On a closer examination of the circumstances I could not but reject this view. Maclean himself was a man, and not a monster, and must have felt or fancied some ground of offence before he constituted himself his wife's executioner ; and in bringing my thoughts to bear upon the woman, I found it impossible to regard one whose fibre physical and mental had held out under a strain such as that known to have been put upon it, as the interesting nullity indicated by the " Senachie " in his account of the event.   The true Elizabeth Campbell, the " Lady of the Rock," must have been not only a woman of high courage, but one who was magnanimously proud.   This last characteristic is to be inferred from the amnesty which, her troubles being over, she is known to have accorded to their authors.   Her marriage to the cowardly savage who was the chief of Mull, her heart being otherwhere engaged, was a political transaction of which she was the tool, yet when the very excess of Maclean's turpitude had given her back to freedom and love, she not only pardons the brother who had bartered her, but pleads for exemption for the traitor who is pretending to mourn her with false tears.

That which unfolded itself to my vision as there I sat, was a royal soul, direct and single, if too passionate to be just ; such an one as might with Cleopatra have cuffed the harmless messenger of evil tidings, and have rewarded with contemptuous favour the doer of her sovereign pleasure.

The part of the Argyle of those days, the third earl, seems to have been that which was generally characteristic of the house—a crafty adoption of the byways most likely to conduct to a safe success.

The malignity everywhere ascribed to the wretched Lachlan Maclean would, but for the acts which justify it, appear overcharged. At once turbulent, cruel, and dull, he was sent at an early age out of reach of the men of his own clan, whose subservience to his vices and disgust at their excess were alike to be feared, to learn discipline and practise knightly exercises among his mother's people in the Clan Chattan. It was through this alliance that the dog of the Maclean arms became quartered with the mountain cat o the MacIntoshes. While with the Clan Chattan he was twice narrowly saved from death at the hands of exasperated retainers. That he failed to command the blind fidelity of service that was common in these clans even towards chiefs who were perhaps as lawless as himself, gives proof of his want of personal influence—a want which is amply accounted for by the absence in this strange being of the physical courage supposed to be the universal inheritance of his class.

Lachlan Maclean succeeded his father in the year 1513. Glutted when he had come into possession by a power which was almost absolute, but which had for him none of the harmonising bonds of a more than brotherly fealty and devotion, his natural defects, as the

years which fostered them succeeded each other, became intensified, and culminated at last in the act
which has prolonged to our own time the reprobation
with which he was regarded in his. But, again, be it
remembered that the man was human, and it is not
to be supposed that this young and fair, this childless
but otherwise unoffending wife, had been sacrificed
by him wholly without motive, especially as the
conservation of her life in full contentment with its
surroundings, was of primal importance to the political object which had been the aim of the alliance.
Since all testimony concurs in showing the Lady
Elizabeth to have been faultless to outward seeming,
the cause which led to her condemnation by Maclean
must be looked for elsewhere than upon the surface,
may be supposed to have resided in some disturbance
of the hidden relations of life, in some secret irritant
or intolerable wound to pride, in some discouragement it might be to nascent passion.

The Argyles as a race are highly strung. This
slender, nervous, bright-haired, quick-witted Campbell was exactly the woman most fitted to awake the
sluggish sense, and to stimulate anything that might
exist of latent sentiment, in such an one as Lachlan
Maclean. That the hold she was likely to obtain over
him should be strong and abiding, belongs to the
fatality by which the more perfect and complex mental

organism must gain upon and ultimately dominate
the lower.   If in the end the brutal nature of the man
reacted against this influence, it would presumably
be in the swell of some counter-current produced by
the presence of an extraneous factor of more than
common strength.   The violated feeling of the woman
seemed to me to account for such a presence.

My thoughts having assigned their parts to Maclean
and his future bride, passed over the stretch of sea
from the castle of Duart to that of Inverary,—went
with the unlikely suitor from Mull to the bright girl
whom the shock of his sudden demand was to startle.
There had been no wooing.   The request for the
already promised hand of Elizabeth Campbell had
been backed by an army of ferocious followers, and
the bargain had been struck before the woman who
would be the suffering party to it was made aware
of its existence.   She did not rebel—the tribal
instinct was too strong within her for that; the clan
demanded from her at her brother's hand the sacrifice
of her life and love, and she made it freely.   Freely,
yes, but with reservation.   What heart might not
rise in sympathy with this long-buried anguish in
reflecting on the cost of an election such as this !
The substitution of one man for another in a maiden's
life is a violence done to every delicate impulse of
her nature; and what a man was this low-browed

Maclean to be palmed on her in place of the Campbell cousin—a man to be qualified only by his likeness to brutes : dogged as a hound, cunning as a cat,
savage as a wolf, and timid as a hare !

The ensign of this nature was freely exhibited ; the
chief who was unloved even of his feudal followers,
could not have been other than ungracious without
as within ; but he was the head of the fighting Clan
Maclean, which the crafty Clan Campbell saw its
interest in propitiating, and she suffered herself to be
accorded to him in bitter silence. It was hard that
she, frail woman as she was, should be given up to
the rude hands, taken to the very heart of the stronghold which the men of her clan had forborne to
withstand or to storm. But she was equal to the
call ; the age-long feud between the Campbells and
Macleans should find the security of a truce in her
person ; but more than this it should not find. She
would bear the odious name, she would sit in the
hated place, leaving the life that had promised so
fair. So much she could accord without soiling her
soul, but in casting out love and its fruition for ever,
she would accept no obscene mockery in its stead :
the place in which the sweet memories of the past
were free as ghosts to come and go, should be pure
of every other presence ; the hostage of her clan,
the strong guardianship of death should save her

from becoming other than in name the wife of the
red Maclean. The woman as I then saw her rose
so strong in her high-hearted reliance on the great
Deliverer, that I fell to thinking with a contempt,
that was not unallied to pity, of the poor creature
who, through all his misery of unappeased longing
and defeated aspiration, could have dared at no
moment of its utmost extremity to confront so stern
a conclusion. I followed him in fancy when his
threats, his pleadings and abasements having served
him nothing, he went forth on the war-path, driven
partly by the necessity of glutting his ire, partly by
the more animating hope of achieving, in the strength
of better men, some shimmer of false glory which
might serve him in his dangerous suit. It was at
this time that the bloody raid was made upon Cairnburg Tower, its owner and its people murdered, and
the castle sacked; and it was now, while hovering
like a bird of prey about the Treshnish Isles, of
which Cairnburg was one, that his acquaintance was
formed with the lady, a daughter of one of his vassal
chiefs, who subsequently became his wife and the
mother of his children. One can hardly wrong the
young girl who courted the favour of Lachlan Maclean,
his hands red with the slaughter of her neighbours,
in attributing to her a cruel, cunning, and sensual
nature, since it is to the latter alone that violence

D

makes welcome appeal; and that this maiden angled successfully for the place she came in time to occupy, the record must be held to at least suggest.

The murderous and predatory exploits of the tyrant of Mull were little likely in any way to move the proud daughter of Argyle. Inured as her mind had been from infancy to tales of blood, of summary vengeance, and all dealings by which the strong hand of the oppressor made itself felt in that day and place, a little more of instinctive loathing would probably be all that the various deeds, by which the chief had thought to impose upon her judgment or her fancy, would procure for him. Her lofty indifference to everything that concerned him, and the passionate absorption of her whole being upon a single point, would make her little likely to constitute herself his judge.

It is acknowledged that the strength of a character is sapped by the vices which derive from it; that the maintenance of a single virtue at a supreme height takes also from available power in other directions, if less generally recognised, is equally true. The armed and vigilant constancy of the lady of Duart would support itself, not without cost, against the direct attack, the ambush, and surprises of these terrible months; the concentrated effort would require the sacrifice of much that was womanly,—and it would have it. My thoughts were in full current, passing from fact to fact, and unconsciously supplying the missing links.

There had come in the life of the red Maclean that crisis which, if it could not lead him to better fortune, could show him the doubly guarded way to it. All that there was of latent sentiment and worthier possibility in this man, would be stirred in the energising vicinity of a nature so full of power and purpose as that of his plighted wife. It would be stirred, but only to expend itself in impotent longing. No worthiest effort would have placed this woman within his reach, and admitting his power of conceiving such, a being so constituted would be utterly incapable of a tension of the will with no reward immediately in view. The lady of high degree, whose life flowed in so deep and silent a current by the side of his turbulent stream, would appear in view of this shallow existence, harassed by its passions and without volume sufficient to urge it on its way, as some cold still lake, into whose depths it was struggling to pour itself. She was as the haven beyond the impassable bar to the foundering mariner, as the last thought of home or hope of heaven to the wretch whose crimes are hurrying him to perdition. Had it been possible that by a woman such as this the past could be forgotten, had there been born in her then the love that hopeth all things,—not the blind Eros, but the clear-

eyed, full-grown, womanly love, the mother of miracles,
—then who shall say that this woman could have
made no way towards the redemption of a human
soul. She had no mind to the work, and the lost
hope, the craven desire, the humiliation, the dumb
rage, and helplessness of his strange defeat, only sunk
him the deeper.   True to the unswerving fidelity
which was the note of her character, that which she
held to be due to him as her part of the compact
between them, was wisely and willingly rendered;
the means she possessed as chatelaine of the castle
were discreetly administered, her firm hand and calm
presence brought order into the lawless household;
and last and most heroic of efforts, the proud spirit
that would be behind-hand in no fraction of its
recognised debt, threw a make-weight even of lighter
cheer into the rude lives amongst which her lot was
cast.   The most faultless of wives to outward seeming, the grief upon which he darkly brooded was
buried in his own dull breast; she consulted his
moods by day, and met their sluggish alternations
with the tact which was inherent in her race.

When Lachlan's hope would faint, and that which
would fain have been love became impotent fury, there
were always at hand savage means for allaying it;
fields to be plundered, ill-defended robbers' nests to be
put under contribution, murder and rapine in countless

forms, all rendered safe for the coward chief by the
strong force to the back and the fore of him, and
secure even from ultimate reprisals under cover of
the shield, which Argyle influence obtained for him
with the king.

Never had the faint heart of Lachlan Maclean,
though rankling under the one unspeakable wrong,
been so swollen with pride. The predatory chiefs on
every side were his vassals, and in his insolent triumph
he hoisted upon Duart tower the ensign of his house,
and made of the Sound of Mull a private water-way,
by firing upon every vessel that failed to lower its
topsails in its honour. His sullen will was supreme
upon all around ; there was one, and one only, whom
it failed to subjugate ; and that one was the woman
who called him lord. When maddened by this unnatural mastery, this victory achieved over him in his
own stronghold, his pride goaded, his senses irritated
beyond the power of bloody deeds to appease, there
were always the smiles of the fair daughter of his
terrified vassal to console him ; and from this harbour
of refuge there dawned upon him one day a plan which
would at once afford him an instalment of revenge,
and seemed to give promise of a more fruitful triumph.
He would take his leman with him to Duart, and set
her in face of the haughty woman who was its mistress.

Dreams, such dreams of power and place as haunt

the brains of sycophants, were busy in the low, tortuous
mind of a creature who could hardly be said to be
fallen, as she made the rough way *en croupe*, steadied
by her hold on the lumbering body of the savagely
expectant Maclean.

The chatelaine received them at the door, and she
looked them through and through with the blue eyes
that had speculation in them, but neither pity nor
reprobation. Her keen wit, bent to a unique point, had
seen a hope in this new combination of circumstance,
a door of relief, possibly of salvation, open from a position of which the strain was a trial which had threat-
ened at times to overmatch her strength.

In the conflict of their separate forces the tyrant
was again worsted ; the calculations of his narrow experience were at fault ; the clear depths of this woman's
soul it was denied to him to cloud. His dull fury
wrought him almost to madness, but working in con-
cert with a more subtle wit, it found ease in inflicting
open insult in return for secret torment.   There came
a time when the complacent mistress took the perilous
place which had been occupied by the hostage ready
to purchase respect at the cost of life, and the fearful
vigil of the lady of Duart was at an end.

If the red Maclean had still hoped that the public
scandal would humiliate his so-called wife, he was
again deceived ; for all change it was apparent that

she pursued her unlovely way of life with a lighter
step, and that her voice had a tenser and a clearer
ring.   His abortive passion had already set him upon
devising strange tortures for its object, he now began
to divert the anguish of his despair in contemplating
means for her destruction which would leave his credit
with her powerful kinsfolk intact.

In this frail and delicate house of clay Maclean
had for the first time come in contact with an
energy which the brutal means at his command were
powerless to subdue ; his efforts to insult and to de-
grade her turned blunted from the fine proof in which
she was armed, and recoiled with force upon himself.
But where he could not wound he might kill ;
"nature's copy in this fair woman" was not "eterne;"
and his thoughts fastening upon this easier, though at
first shadowy, alternative, the way to it became gradually cleared.   For it happened that in the meanwhile
the thoughts of his frail partner had not been idle.
The lady who ruled with so even a hand the affairs of
Castle Duart, and was an object of reverential respect,
not only to its female dependants but to the last and
lowest of its train of savage freebooters, whose purity
was untouched by a feeling in relation to the minion
of Maclean other than a grateful sense of the relief,
which her presence had procured—this high-born
lady whose foot seemed unconsciously to tread her

down, could not fail to attract to herself all that existed of vindictive capacity in the little soul that waxed sickly and seemed to grow less in her shadow.   Nor was the feeling, that gained possession of the latter, only the natural repulsion of dark and crooked things for clear and straight : the existence of the lawful wife was a bar over which her low ambition could not vault.   Her hands had not been swift to shed blood, nor her voice to command its shedding, as those of her paramour, and her less familiar thought, inactive as regards the means, dwelt only on the desired end. But that end was perpetually before her, and ignorant and superstitious, as she was malignant and feeble, she tried to speed it in a manner much affected by spirits of her class in that day.

Having made an image of wax in the likeness, as far as she was able, of the scornful woman who was the obstacle in her path, she pleased her fancy, and ministered to a wild hope, in piercing, pricking, and otherwise outraging the simulacre, while she chanted over it an incantation which should incite the powers of evil to do the like by her living foe.   The leman is found by Maclean in her chamber, crooning the spell over the waxen likeness of his wife, and the dull, long seething thought is kindled within him, and trans-ferred in a look of their meeting eyes, to the motherly keeping of the woman.   Both shrink at first from the

horrible conclusion they have seen mirrored in each
other's glances, but the shamefacedness with which
they have recognised this progeny of sin has quickly
passed, and dark hints concerning it are formulated by
their lips. The dull blood of Lachlan Maclean has
not been crossed for nothing with the sharper current
derived through his mother, and a gleam of cat-like
cunning shows him the use to which this outcome of
their conjoined desire may be turned. Shrouded and
veiled as the fair Campbell had been at her bridal, this
ghastly image, waxen white and deadly calm, taken
for burial to Inverary, would give assurance of the
peaceful death of her in whose likeness it was made.
A funeral train composed of every fighting man of the
Clan Maclean would follow, and the well-dissembled
grief of the arch-traitor at their head, would be a bond
of present sympathy between the chiefs of the two
clans ; and the alliance having done him good service in the past, the future might take care of itself.

But the ways and means by which the end of the
doomed woman was to be composed, required grave
reflections.

It was no easy matter to do away with one who
possessed the goodwill of an entire clan. The deed
could hardly be accomplished within the Castle. The
confederates sought each other's society continually,
and discussed their several plans while keeping uneasy

watch, parting company at the singing of a scullion over his work, or the entrance of a bat through a loop-hole.   Daunted by the shadow of coming guilt, they would fly asunder, each to watch from separate win-dows the closing in of night or the signs of gathering storm ; they would hide when there was nobody to see, and would speak under their breath when there was nobody to hear.   They often——

"You are listening to the whispers that are all about the place.   It is a wonder to a stranger to hear them, and the wind so still."

I had been so lost in my thoughts that I was startled as at the sudden appearance of the phantoms I had been invoking.   The revulsion would have been less sudden, the surprise for the moment hardly greater, had I met on looking up the dull glow of the blood-shot eyes and shaggy beard of the red Maclean.   As it was, a figure of a very different type came between me and the warp that my fancy had been weaving upon the woof of fact.

The man who stood at rest upon one foot within two yards of me as I sat and looked dreamily out upon the sea through my chosen window-place, was of the middle height, lightly and slenderly made, with a small head, steep brow, well-finished ears and nostrils, and eyes which, brown and clear as a moun-tain brook, had a touch of sadness in their lingering gaze. His figure was so light, and the drawing of his features so clear, that before noting the plentiful white threads in his still dark hair, and the fine lines on the surface of his skin, I had taken him for a youth. The words I had heard were not the first he had addressed to me, and on his repeating the summons from Helmuth, which he had been sent to deliver, I succeeded in identifying him with our future host—the "lad" of whom Miss Macorquodale had more than once spoken. As we went together to the cottage, he resumed of his own accord the subject of the mysterious sounds, the objective nature of which I had been half inclined to doubt, until I found that they spoke to this man as they had done to me, not always in guilty whispers, but sometimes in short sobs, in low sudden ejaculations, shivering sighs, in love-plaints long drawn out, all ending in the dull, merciless laugh which I had heard more than once, and each time with a growing sense of dread and repulsion. It was as if the ghosts of all the passions, stormy or tender, violent or treacherous, which had stirred living men and women in this place, were wandering about it in cold unrest.

There was little to be made of these fantastic echoes, and I took occasion to inquire of Archie Cumming if the Hills of the Two Winds, of which mention had been made by the veteran soldier, were to be

seen from hence.   He pointed them out to me as
they rose behind Mr. Guthrie's park and beyond
Craigienure, dark against that part of the sky towards which the now sinking sun was tending, and
it chanced that the appearance, which had procured
them their Gaelic name, was manifest at this moment.
Driven by opposing currents, a column of vapour,
whose larger base seemed to sweep round that of the
twin hills, went up between them, grey upon the
yellowing clearness, like a shaft of smoke into the
lighter air ; but there was no time to linger over this
strange effect, the hospitably entertained nag from
Craigienure had been put to, and a rough if not
long drive was before us.

Miss Macorquodale was eager in her desire to
ascertain what more could be done for our comfort
in the good time that was coming,—what we should
like to eat, and at what hours we would eat it.

" Mutton, Miss Macorquodale ; there is nothing so
good as mutton."   This was said by a man who
knows not whether he eats mutton or beef, but who,
seeing sheep to be plentiful in these parts, believed
that he was making things easy.

Miss Macorquodale gave utterance to a long-
sustained " O—h ! " along which her thoughts seemed
slowly travelling in search of the required provender,
but brightening as they reached Oban, she continued

smiling : " Fresh meat,—of course you will want fresh meat, and when will you have it whatefer ? "

" Nothing for breakfast but your good new-laid eggs and a little bacon, and just a few cutlets at half-past one."

" Yes, cutlets the first day," rejoined Miss Macorquodale cheerfully, " and then a shoulder, a chicken in between, and then the leg ; oh yes, it will keep, I have a beautiful place for keeping it." She had been contemplating in fancy the side of mutton brought from Oban, and saw her way to its conservation.

" Not so extravagant, Miss Macorquodale," I cried, seeing all that was available being used up for lunch ; " you must keep something back for dinner, we shall want it at seven."

" You will dine twice in the day, dear," said our poor purveyor, for the moment evidently taken aback; but her thoughts returning along the now familiar way to Oban, she became once more confident in its resources. " You will dine twice a day," she repeated affirmatively, " in course—I know ;—it iss the quality's ways ; and why for should you not dine three times if you could anyway get to fancy it ? "

But there was no further surprise in store for Miss Macorquodale or tax upon her ingenuity ; we did not threaten to call for unattainable delicacies in the dead of the night ; and having given into my hand a basket of butter wrapped in immaculate muslin, she saw us depart, if with cheerful visions of our return, with, I think, a little sigh of present relief.

If the sitting-room of the Craigienure Inn, wherein our table was spread for dinner, presented as cheery an aspect as it had done the day before, our belief in the wisdom of the change we contemplated was enforced by finding that we could not possess it to ourselves. The covers were just about to be removed by the red-armed maid, when the door opened, and a young man who hesitated and seemed somewhat dis-countenanced by our presence, made his appearance. Glancing at the table, we saw what we had not noted before, that it was laid for three, and understanding the position of affairs at once, we made the modest stranger welcome to what we now saw was the public room. He was clearly a gentleman, and the chance companionship turned out in the end to be pleasant. He had come to Mull with a view to taking a part of the shooting of Loch Buy, the laird in whose company we had crossed from Oban.

The tide of civilisation, with the frothy elements that it bears upon its surface, had seemed when it first reached these remote Highlands, to intoxicate the un-seasoned heads of the Scottish chiefs, who, plunged into the current, were soon drawn towards London;

where a large moiety of them dissipated their fortunes, and compromised the future of their faithful dependants, in every species of excess. What had happened to others, had happened to the Macleans, and the Loch Buy branch were still feeling the pressure of the burden then laid upon the estate, though eased in the present generation by a wealthy marriage. Our new acquaintance was fresh from an inspection of the moor, the wild beauty of which had greatly taken his fancy. He was to return on the morrow for a visit of some days to the hospitable chief, with whom he then hoped to conclude the treaty, making the shooting and the lodge his own, for the term of years intervening between the present date and the coming of age of the little laird, the Loch Buy of the future. As it was chiefly grouse, and not deer either red or roe, upon which the heart of our sanguine table-companion was set, it is to be hoped that he is not now lamenting over his bargain, for I hear that even in drier seasons, very little grouse is to be met with in Mull, and next to none at all at Loch Buy.

We made the best of the fair weather of the next few days, and kept the Craigienure trap in pretty constant requisition. First we visited Moy Castle, which is also on Loch Buy, driving past Loch Spelve, the home of innumerable sea-fowl, and Loch Uisk, where the character of the scenery changes, the hills

closing in on the right, and becoming richly wooded.
It is to be hoped that the buried generations of Macleans of a junior branch who inhabited this tower,
were tolerably at peace among themselves, for they
had close quarters in which to settle their grievances.

We saw the little daughter of the house, who
asked after the health and good cheer of her god-
child in a tone as of one who held us responsible
for it; and we accosted a man, evidently a factotum
of the family, who left his present business of curing
fish, to show us over the tower. The dungeons of
this little hornet's nest were a conspicuous feature,
and as they occupied nearly the whole of the foundation, the groans of the victims rotting in their un-
wholesome depths must have gone up to the ears of the
victorious Macleans as a sweet sacrifice continually.

On following days when the weather permitted, and
we were not particular, we took other directions;
once skirting the coast along the Sound of Mull, and
once going by Strachdale towards Loch-na-Kiel,
which I greatly wished to reach; but the road becoming impassable for wheels, we had to turn off
to the left. From a pleasure trip round the Island
of Mull in Mr. Guthrie's yacht, I excused myself,
glad for once of a long day alone, for I had work
on hand which had been carrying itself on, I scarce
know how, but chiefly at odd moments in the long

drives when the loneliness of the scenes made us silent. For Mull is very lonely of human presence, and in view of the scantiness of its population we often thought of the old soldier who longed to labour its idle soil, and to taste of its unbreathed air. As we came to know it, and the subtle qualities of its beauty had time to penetrate—for the special loveliness of the Highlands of Scotland is an educational instrument—we well understood the hold which his early home still laid upon his heart, and were less inclined than ever to acquiesce in a system which kept it so unproductive.

By the day on which, true to our engagement this time, we started with our belongings for Duart, a good deal of paper, which according to the German proverb is patient, was written over in lines of various lengths : in short, the work on which I had been engaged at odd times was a poem having for its subject the story of the Lady of the Rock. I was returning to the spot with a sense of peculiar pleasure, my thoughts having been hanging about it with such persistence ; for the inditing of a poem, and especially when a story takes to singing itself, is a process after the manner of an incantation to which the singer is driven in order to "lay"—to exorcise from the mind—a haunting idea.

As we grow to love some new aspect of nature, to

E

take an interest in some new soil, we naturally become
curious and eager about the people to whose being,
physical and moral, it has ministered, and more
especially are we solicitous to make acquaintance
with those who may be regarded as its most typical
products.   We went therefore from Craigienure
furnished by the kind minister of its little church with
the names and addresses of two old people whose
dwelling lay between Craigienure and Duart.   In
the first cottage with a slated roof, on the road
branching to the left from the highway to Auchnacraig, lived Niel Lamond, an ex-bailiff whose conduct
had won him respect, and the humble competence
which I fear he could hardly be said to enjoy.   We
sighted the old man where he sat under the shelter
of a hay-rick, for we had come through the wood and
parted company with trees, indeed, with all vegetation
that was taller than a quite unmiraculous beanstalk.
We drew up by the side of the road and addressed
him by name, when he rose with some little difficulty,
and came towards us, feeling his way to the sound
of our voices with his stick.   As he stood before us,
his eyes, which were light in colour but ringed like
an agate, looked blankly beside our faces, and we
saw that he was blind.   He had no human fellowship
that we could perceive, for the cottage had an empty
look ; a cow and a donkey whose aimless steps he

may have heard with the crunching of the crisp grass, and the sunbeams which the cold wind rendered less than tepid, for all environment. The waste emptiness of this life was oppressive to the imagination, and we would have lingered longer in the hope of affording a momentary relief to its monotony, had we felt sure that the interruption was welcome. As it was, the thoughts of the blind man—and he must have had many, sitting and mooning about day after day in the dark— seemed to have difficulty in finding their way to his lips, and the needed effort to give him little pleasure. The slow current was, however, somewhat quickened when we led him upon by-gone days. Ten families, he told us, ten families of farmers, more or less well to do, had dwelt between the spot where we stood and that where the road takes off from the highway to Auchnacraig, and where, as we had observed, not so much as the ruin of a human habitation was now to be seen. Mull was not then as it is to-day; there were sons and daughters in those uprooted home-steads, strong men and bonny maids as you could find in all Scotland. The old man's face lightened a little as he spoke; he had come upon days before the world had grown dark. It was the old story of the men trodden out by the deer; it met us wher-ever we went, and appeared a somewhat ironical rendering of the law of the survival of the fittest.

We bade Niel Lamond adieu when the faint flicker of memory had died down, and left him to his neighbourless solitude. For neighbours in the sense of companions he could hardly have found in the three women who occupied the bothies standing side by side on the moor a little farther to the left.

It was to Susan MacArthur, the very ancient dame who dwelt alone in the first, that we had been recommended to address ourselves after leaving Niel Lamond. Her door was closed, and the bothy seeming tenantless, we knocked at the door farther on, and after a slight delay, saw ourselves cautiously inspected from a gradually widening chink, by an eye whose owner was evidently labouring under a suspense of opinion in regard to us. The why and wherefore of such uncalled-for appearances was a problem too unaccustomed to be other than troublous, and the habit of mind imparted by the treacherous climate to Highland and Lowland Scot alike, leads them to prefer their own conclusions to the doubtful evidence of strangers, witnessing to their own intentions. We asked after Susan MacArthur; did she live in the neighbouring bothy?

"An' if she do, what might it be ye may want wi' her?" asked the owner of the eye, at the same time bringing up its fellow to reinforce it.

"We have been told that Mrs. MacArthur knows

a great deal about Mull that we should like to hear, and we were passing, and wished to pay her a visit."

There was clearly nothing in this that was necessarily reassuring, but the very witlessness of the make-believe, if make-believe it were, brought contempt for our powers of mischief, and the chink in the door became sensibly wider.

"She'll no be in the day. Be ye living in these pairts?"

"We are coming to live at Duart Farm."

"Oh, ye be they that are coming to Duart Farm?" and curiosity getting the better of prudence, the hinge yet further relaxed. While the wary door-keeper was inspecting our persons with greater convenience to herself, we also took occasion to examine hers. On her head, growing low upon a brow square as that of a Highland bull, was a shock of hair as tawny-brown as is commonly the colour of its coat, and the resemblance was further carried out in the unkempt wildness of the woman's whole appearance, and its promise of compact strength. The eyes that were reading us so cautiously were very bright, and a smile which before we had done we succeeded in eliciting, showed teeth so short and even, beneath the healthy gums, as to unsettle the ideas of her age which we had derived from her weather-beaten skin. Her two hands, one of which held the door, and the

other the lintel, were at this moment snow white,
being covered to the wrists with a coating of flour
and water, which she accounted for by telling us she
was making scones for her mother's tea.

"Oh, you live here with your mother,—is she old?"

"No so fery that; somewhere at the back o'
eighty."

To us that term of years seemed not contemptible,
and we felt we should have liked to make the old
lady's acquaintance.

"Does your mother object to see strangers?"

"She's no well the day, and hasna left her bed,"
and the hands that had been engaged in the old
woman's service began picking at the coating of
rapidly drying dough, and were assuming, where
divested of that integument, the grey colour of wood
ashes. The interior of the bothy with its window
of no more than a foot square, seemed very dark,
and I felt sorry for the sick mother who was about
to partake by faith and not by sight of the mess
which was in preparation for her. The contrast of
colour seemed not to strike our new acquaintance,
and we could only hope as we bid her good-bye that
the ground tint of her hands might prove faster than
the superficial.

As we proceeded on our way, having regained the
"machine," we came to a part where the still seem-

ingly common land was enclosed by a dyke, and saw, labouring towards us on the other side of the road crossed by a gate, a small frail figure leaning on a stick, very heavily shod, and bending under the weight of several burthens in addition to the crowning one of years. The wayfarer was a little old woman, who being close upon the gate, deposited as much of her load as she could ever hope to ease herself of on this side time, upon the roadside, and opened for us to pass with the fussy eagerness of age, glad to feel itself of some small use. The gate was heavy and ill hung, and Helmuth having got down from the trap, his stronger hand helped her to perform this service. A little knotty fist bore hard upon the stick, as the old woman exacted from her refractory knees a series of curtseys. Sure, in spite of the discouraging statement of her neighbour, that we had come upon Susan MacArthur, I also descended from the dog-cart. The old woman, much bent, and trembling a little at the unexpected encounter, turned from one to the other of us a face whereof the eyes had so much of latent youth in them, and so wistful a look withal, that we could have imagined her to be some young spirit bound to this withered body by an evil spell. The clear eyes that looked at us from their wrinkled surroundings, were blue and very soft and kind; the chiselling of the brow and nose still delicate ; the furrowed skin so far as this, still fair, only below it all was havoc and devasta- tion. Half ashamed of our height and the able- bodied strength of which we made so little proportion- ate use, we stood over that saddest sight to mortal eyes, a human ruin—a sight more sad in the present instance by reason of the evident beauty upon which the cruel tooth of time had preyed. Most melancholy perhaps of all is the little reverence that destitute old age appears to feel for itself, there being some- thing deprecatory, almost abject, in its attitude to- wards those in present effective possession of the field of time—as of a visitor conscious of having outstood his welcome. It was indeed Susan Mac- Arthur whom we had met, returning from the visit which she made once or twice a week in all weathers —barring a too high wind—to the good Miss Mac- orquodale, who never suffered her to depart empty- handed.

It was not difficult to get the old woman to talk ; she abounded in information, and was glad to give it forth. She had long passed the limit of human life, being turned of ninety-three, and had seen six generations of her forbears, her children, and children's children—most of them buried in Auchna- craig kirkyard, though some were now living beyond the seas. It was not the same world that it used to be, people seemed to be dying out so, that it felt to be quite lonesome to be going about in it. There were cottages and gardens all along where you stood in the old days, and dancing to the pipes every week in Duart Tower, reels and strathspeys; it was a wonder to see the lads and the lassies how they sprung, and she as high as any, but she could not do it now. There was a roof on Duart Tower then, and a floor, such a floor for dancing as was not in all Mull beside; but there came a dishonest factor, and no one living at the Hall, and he sold the timber and put it in his own pocket and none the wiser, only a great many people the duller for the want of the dancing. Now there was no one to dance if the Queen herself should lay down a floor.

Was it poetry that we wished to hear? There was a great deal of poetry going about in those brighter days; her own mother was a rare hand at it, and she herself had never need to hear a piece that took her fancy more than twice before she got it by heart. Yes, she would say it to us as much as we liked, but had we got the Gaelic? That was a pity; but she had the English too, only there was not so much poetry made in English as in Gaelic.

We helped to settle her loaf, her can of milk, and her various smaller parcels upon her, and we parted on the understanding that she was to come to see us

at the farm—an arrangement that she held to in pre-
ference to our going to see her, partly perhaps that
she liked the change of scene, partly that such visits
were known to be profitable. A little donation that
Helmuth put into her trembling hand was acknowledged by a sad succession of curtseys, by a young
smile of the uplifted eyes, and a toothless laugh of
the devastated mouth.

We found Miss Macorquodale and her little dog at
the door, both overflowing with welcome, for Flora,
with the quick instinct of her kind, had soon discovered who it was that her mistress delighted to
honour. Miss Macorquodale, who could not see
people five minutes in her house without eating her
salt in one fashion or another, had been exercised in
her mind on the subject of tea, not knowing where
that meal ought to stand in relation to the two
dinners. We made her happy by asking for it on the
spot, and she was at once active in its preparation.

As with a pile of newly-made "baps" she followed her maid with the kettle, she found me examining a very heterogeneous pile of books, ranked
against the wall on a side-table. The week of bad
weather at Oban, and the subsequent evenings at
Craigienure, had pretty nearly exhausted my small
travelling supply, and I was hovering over this un-
promising field, resolved not to be dainty.

"There iss books to last the life o' anybody that iss given to the reading o' them," said Miss Macorquodale, " poetry, and history—all that ever can be thought of. It iss the lad that iss so mad for study, blinding himself with the print, and especially the poetry that seems to go chiming in his head like a bell that has been pulled too hard, when he'd be better in bed and dreaming of his crops."

With increased hope I resumed my investigations, and found that the collection which ministered to the ideal element in the mind of the farmer, consisted of two, Bibles, one in English, the other in Gaelic; of Drelincourt's " Consolations against the Fears of Death," commended by the testimony of Mrs. Veal's ghost; of Walter Scott's " Monastery," " Marmion," " Last Minstrel," and " Lord of the Isles "—evidently picked up at odd times, being in various editions; of " The Mysteries of Udolfo," the " Pilgrim's Progress," an anthology with the title of the " Little Warbler," a hymn-book, and odd numbers of several periodicals, in one of which I fastened upon an account of the miraculous building and nature of the Great Pyramid, and was lost for a time—the Celtic part of me at least—in the enjoyment of the supernatural.

The chance juxtaposition of books in such quarters is always curious, and often suggestive. In the present instance the narrative of the very material ghost of Mrs. Veal (who might as well have been Mrs. Beef) resting upon that of the transcendental origin of the solidest mass of masonry on the face of the earth, while establishing its own existence by reference to the dark secret of the scoured gown of Mrs. Bardel, seemed each to lend a point of irony to the other.

When we returned from our walk to Loch Don, in which Archie Cumming in his best clothes had been our guide, we found our table in course of arrangement by the maid of the farm, while Miss Macorquodale was busy in the kitchen providing for the wants of the carnivorous creatures she had taken into her kindly keeping. The girl, who was as shy as a young fox, incontinently let fall the contents of her hands on our appearance, and the rattling of the knives and forks overpowering her failing efforts at self-control, she threw up her apron, and rushed, covered with confusion, from the room. And yet in that moment we had seen that the lassie so fearful of observation was one who might well have repaid it. Her silky hair was the colour of a chestnut fresh from the pod; the glance of her brown eyes was as gentle as it was shy; her skin had on it a wonderful sheen of health; and the well-expanded lungs beneath the ungirt chest and waist, lent a rare purity to the blush with which her cheeks were dyed. Many a time during the first trying ordeal of that to her seemingly uncanny candle-light dinner, did she nerve herself to return upon the scene, bearing the dishes or implements with which she had been charged; but never on that occasion did she succeed in setting what she carried in its rightful place, the wave of resolution breaking each time somewhere short of this final consummation. We made up her short-comings in her moments of retreat, and endeavoured to look as innocent of our share in the performance as if the work had been done by " brownies." For the rest, we missed nothing in our new quarters that was essential to our well-being, and enjoyed for a time a measure of solitude, a room to breathe and to be in, hitherto unknown in our existence.

A large portion of my time was spent in Duart Castle, sitting in my old place on the window stone. It was there I wrote, filling in with the renewed impulse imparted by my surroundings, the spaces that had been left vacant in my Rhyme of the Lady of the Rock. I had finished my record, had given out all that was in me, was feeling my emptiness, and endeavouring to relax the recent tension by spreading myself out as it were, lying passive to external influence, when, putting to flight the echoes that were again becoming busy in spite of me, I heard

a familiar step. It was Helmuth, who had sought
me here on his return from his morning walk. I
showed him my finished manuscript. " It has done
itself," I said, "with the help of the echoes ; and
now I have had enough of them. I don't want to
hear them any more."

" You should read me what you have written ; it
is the likeliest way to lay them."

At the moment I hardly thought so, and it needed
some persuasion to induce me to return upon the
track of my thoughts, even in the company of that
only one of whom I have ever taken counsel by the
way. Let no one conversant of the manners of
singers smile, incredulous of any difficulty in such a
matter. Never since I printed my first page have
I shared the seemingly common desire to test the
effect of my performance orally on individuals. The
work once thrown off, I feel my part in it at an end,
and commit it to the waters, launch the paper boat
freighted with my thought to take its chance with
the stream,—be wrecked at the first onset, or borne
God only knows how far. Should any one have
succeeded in making concrete a just idea, that idea
so embodied will have become as a seed whose life
is in itself, and in its day and hour, if ever it have
a day or an hour, it will bring forth fruit after its
kind. Many a thrifty germ perishes for the want

of favouring conditions, but I am persuaded that
it is beyond the power of human foresight to
bring it into contact with such. Probably few
works that do not either borrow adventitious aid
from some exaggerated mode of the hour, or syn-
chronise with the turn of the tide when it sets in
against it, are likely to be greeted with contem-
porary acclaim; but such influences are short-lived,
and liable to fatal reaction. And if the normal
course of that social evolution which bears upon a
work of art is difficult to calculate, what shall be
said of the cataclysms and storms which may over-
take it, and of the abiding presence of a variety of
superficial phenomena, each of which might suffice
to the destruction of creations possessed of infinite
fecundity? The dust which the traveller shakes from
his feet at Olympia may have served to make visible
thoughts as precious as those embodied for posterity
in the Hermes of Praxeteles; we know indeed that
it has been so; but we may also safely infer that
many a no less vital idea has perished and left, not
only no record of itself, but none even of the hand
which sought to put it on record. God grant that
the many nameless "makers" who have lived and
died, have not been defrauded of their joy in the
exercise of faculty. If it has been theirs in sufficient
measure, they have had their reward; for I persist

in spite of all altruistic argument to the contrary, in regarding happiness as an end in itself, albeit it is one for which personally it is lost labour to work.

Our thoughts did not take so wide a sweep at the time; they were centred in the spot, for I was doing as I was desired, reading my poem in the place where it was made. Never again will it have such an auditor, and never again in all probability will it be made vocal in this place. All chances had conspired to the vividness of the impression, and to the disarming of the criticism which I redoubted, knowing of old how it imposed itself by its justice and good faith. I knew that the circumstances were in my favour, but forbearing too closely to question their part in the result, I took this best first-fruit of my labours, and was thankful.

The following morning there came a discreet knock at our sitting-room door, which was opened at my invitation by our Highland Hebe, sent by Miss Macorquodale to tell me that Susan MacArthur was in the house-place. I went at once, and found the old woman seated in the middle of the room with a can of milk and a well-filled basket at her side, and with a plate on her lap from which she was taking the refection that was the fatality of the house. She set the plate upon a chair that had been placed beside her for my use—it was evident the little scene had been dramatically arranged—and she was about to seek the assistance of her stick in the execution of her numerous curtseys, when I took her hand. The clear, blue, up-turned eyes were brighter than before, and in addition to their wistful, questioning gaze, there was a little sparkle of humour not perceptible at our first meeting. For the rest, the mockery of the young glance that seemed trying to pierce its way through the wreck seemed even more cruel, seen as it now was in contrast with the freshness and youthful strength so gravely put forth of the girl who passed to and fro on her way to the hearth, bearing with ease a pile of logs which might have taxed the powers of a drayman, and lifting and rearranging the vast pots and kettles, which hung over the wood fire, with the celerity of a child dealing with its toys.

There is something in a kitchen which is apt to carry a suggestion of childish days. Is it that the goodwill of a cook is able to clothe itself in forms so universally popular? Whatever the reason, the association with childhood may be held to be the sufficient cause of its permanent charm. But a kitchen also commends itself on wider grounds. No other room—excepting perhaps a nursery—can compete with it in its air of comfort; and as all its resplendent adornments from the dredger to the warming-pan

F

are objects of use, no other apartment whatever is so
wholly removed from vulgar pretence, and so safe
therefore in its appeal to a fastidious taste.

Miss Macorquodale's kitchen in particular was
like one in a fairy-tale, the old woman in its midst
being the fairy.   Animals living in familiar relationship with man had got to be so very knowing that
the familiarity occasionally bred contempt.   A cat
stretched before the fire would hardly budge for any
one ; a keen-eyed hen came fluttering in from time
to time, snatching a morsel even from the plate ; a
speculative pig regarded the windfalls on the floor
as his proper perquisites ; and the little dog Flora,
the child of the house, was generally in undisputed
possession of the best arm-chair.

Seeing that Miss Macorquodale was engaged by
the front window upon some work which appeared
to occupy much of her attention, I crossed over to
her, and found that she was gingerly rubbing, with
fingers that looked too nice for the work, one of the
cork-soled boots that I had worn on the muddy walk
of the day before.   On the window-sill stood its
fellow, and a cup half full of milk which she had
been applying with a sponge, and near by, a saucer
containing what but a pat of her own dainty butter !
It was this last which she was enduring to see now,
and with her own hand, put to this basest of uses. .

"Dear Miss Macorquodale," I exclaimed, shocked at the spectacle, "you are not satisfied with spoiling me, you are going now positively to spoil my boots."

"How would you have me do?" asked Miss Macorquodale, looking from one to the other of them with a face of grave concern; "the butter can no hurt them—it will do them good—fresh churned butter, and the milk new from the cow."

The hospitality of this Highland woman was clearly incorrigible; I gave up the attempt to restrain it in despair. I had scarcely satisfied her that it was not the destruction of my property that I deprecated, when Helmuth found his way into the kitchen, and having renewed his acquaintance with Susan Mac-Arthur, made a stand like a pointer discerning fresh game, in the direction of a figure of which I had as yet become scarcely cognisant.

The foreign element in the little company which had attracted his quick eye appeared in the person of a man who, seated at a small table placed against a window overlooking the Castle, was fully occupied at this moment in the silent despatch of what seemed to be a very copious breakfast. The stranger was about forty-five, way-worn and travel-soiled; his figure small and lean, his features insignificant; his iron-grey locks sparsely covering a large head very flat at the summit and wide at the sides; his hard

eye, his rusty garb, and a look which seemed to invite
the knocks of fate while it promised a sharp retort to
them, gave me the fantastic notion in regard to him
that he resembled a nail out of service. A pedlar's
pack was resting against the wall at his side, and on
a chair near at hand, a tray on which were displayed
the various small wares, the laces, combs, and such
like, of the itinerant merchant. The meal spread
before him was not only abundant and of the best,
but it was set forth with all the homely refinement
of which the place was capable; a fair white cloth
on the board, and everything bright and well ordered.
While Helmuth was beginning an acquaintance with
the stranger, whose accent showed him to be not of
this country, Miss Macorquodale came up to reinforce
the repast with an excellent cheese, and stood beaming approval upon her new guest as he cut from it
large slices, and, the edge of an indiscriminating
hunger having been taken off, ate them with leisurely
gusto in the intervals of conversation. He was a
Swiss, from the Canton Zürich; had left his home
at the age of twenty, and had tramped about the
world scores, hundreds, thousands of miles in all
those weary years, and found no comfort and little
rest. He had been driven from home by the tyranny
of his father, a masterful, prosperous man who had
made his own way in life, and wanted to bend or to

break all who fell under his hand to his own conditions, and confine them in the groove that had fitted himself. His violent cruelty had so wrought upon a more tender-spirited brother that the youth had put an end to his existence. As we listened to the strange pedlar, a vivid picture of the unnatural warfare of that home among the Alps rose up before us, for it was clear that this one at least of the tyrant's sons had inherited some of the stormy passions of the father, the looks that he directed towards us and his incisive tones being full of a wrath that the years had not sufficed wholly to quench. The harsh parent had, however, given him a good education; he was speaking excellent German for a Swiss, with a rather pedantic choiceness of diction, and was not disinclined to boast of the learning obtained, as he said, at a university, which was the only solace of his lonely life. Full of commiseration for a fate of such peculiar hardship, and stimulated perhaps by an unconscious desire to escape from the accusing gaze which seemed to confound us with the author of his misfortunes, Helmuth conceived the happy idea of buying the contents of the hawker's tray, and distributing them between Susan MacArthur, Miss Macorquodale, and her maid, Maisie.

While the above division was in progress, I returned to my old fairy, who had finished her cakes and milk; and there being no fear of any one perishing from inanition for the present, we were suffered by Miss Macorquodale to enter upon what for me was the business of the meeting.   Susan MacArthur had come fully understanding what was expected of her, and was seemingly too acknowledged a mistress of her art, to experience either shyness or hesitation.

"It's a pity to be sure that ye'll no hae the Gaelic; it's in the Gaelic that the pick o' the songs is to be found."

I thought she would be more at home at first going off in the, to me, unknown tongue, and said that although I could not understand the sense, I should like to hear the sound of it.

Suddenly, in prompt reply to my words, the old woman straightened herself upon her chair, looked before her, as though she could see through the intervening walls into some far past or misty future, and there arose in the place a thin thread of quavering sound, high and even shrill in parts, at times unutterably mournful, but not without variety of expression, nor wholly wanting in sweetness and tune.   To the surprise of my ignorance, old Susan was not reciting but singing the ditty whose dramatic changes I could only guess by the acceleration or relenting of the time, the quick taking of the breath, the pauses, frequently so eloquent, and the occasional furtive glance from the corner of her eye, to see how the spell was working. It worked well, for many circumstances were conducing to its effect. The sky, which in the early morning had held out a false promise of fair weather, was rapidly overclouding, while the wind, rising in short gusty sobs, brought an occasional shower of sleet against the window-panes, as if some uneasy elemental spirit was trying to call our attention to its perturbation. Softer and less near at hand, the measured boom of the rising tide made a deep and firm orchestral accompaniment to the tremulous and shrill solo that was shaking itself out upon it.

The song subsided as suddenly as the high-pitched tones of a clock that has told the hour and has no more to say. The Sibylline expression had departed from the old woman's countenance, and the rigidity from her frame; her mouth resumed its aimless working, and her figure its attitude of feeble maundering. But the spell still lingered. There had been a strange power in the weird notes, and the, by us only dimly surmised, words which had probably stirred so many simple hearts, and which were evidently potent still, as might be gathered from the soft, suffused glance of Maisie, who, peeling potatoes at the dresser, turned her eyes from time to time in the direction of the ancient singer. I was sensible of my loss in not "having the Gaelic," and in order to be more even with Maisie (the heart of Miss Macorquodale was harder on the side of poetry), I begged to be favoured by Susan with some morsel, albeit less choice, in the inferior tongue. The old woman turned over her stock with the assistance of our hostess. She did not as before seem to gather her singing robes about her, but prefaced the performance with a little half-waggish, half-deprecating chuckle.

On the whole we were not gainers by the change of medium. The English songs, retained by Susan from the repertory of her mother, were not truly ancient, and had, as she had well seen, little to commend them as poetry; the vague suggestion of the Gaelic had been better.

But the scene itself was full of poetic elements; we were such a strange company brought together from different parts, and furnishing samples of humanity under varied aspects. There was the kindly old Sibyl who was the centre of the group, crooning out the songs of other days; there was the woman-singer trying to select some accordant notes from among the discords which smote her heart in these; a little removed, in the fresh charm of her expanding womanhood, stood the peasant girl, the daughter of a race more tensely strung than ours. Slightly in advance of her sat the man from the German Fatherland, who, loving his country with an unalterable love, had yet struck the roots of a prosperous life deep down in the England of his adoption ; and near him was that other man from the Alps, dwelling in bitterness of spirit on the scenes of his youth while passing his days as a homeless wanderer in a land that continued to be alien. Last, but not least, there stood—looking from one to the other of us with an odd sort of pride as of possession—the old maid with the mother's heart, too busy with our material needs to take personal part in our intellectual refreshment, but glad that in the intervals of graver concern, we were able to amuse ourselves with such harmless trifling.

The pedlar had finished his meal, and, sensible of having done a good business, was in no hurry to shoulder his pack and depart for Tobermory, but sat bending forward, enjoying the comfort of his present quarters, and the opportunity afforded by the performance that was in progress for superior criticism.

> "There was a miller's daughter,
>   And young and fair was she;
> A squire's son he sought her
>   His true-love for to be.
>   Tairy-airy, tum tum tairy,
>   Tairy-airy, tum tum de;"

sung the old woman; and the face and attitude of the itinerant chapman clearly told us how very cheap he

held her song.   But her back was turned to him ; it
was another part of her audience that she addressed,
and she evidently enjoyed the smiles which greeted
the droll burthen affording her such a convenient
halting-place for calling up the stray forces of memory.
When the sorrows and ultimate triumph of the Miller's
Daughter had been followed up throughout some
score of verses, each one ending with the tag, we
were anxious to learn how and when the venerable
singer had become possessed of the song.   It proved
to have been one picked up by the musical mother
from whom Susan inherited her faculty, in a visit made
in her young days to Tobermory ; the words had been
sung in the village street by an itinerant like our Swiss
friend, who had been able thus to recommend his mer-
chandise—for he had had copies of the ballad in print.

" These modern *Volks-Lieder*—what you may call
—of the English and English-speaking Scotch have
no value at all, poetical or archæologish," put in the
pedlar ; "my pack is heavy with the stuff, for I am
asked for it wherever I go, but I like better to sell
scissors and knives."

We all, with the exception of old Susan, looked at
him ; his voice, sharp as his favourite ware, seemed
to have severed some chord, and to have disturbed
the harmony.   We were silent, not wishing to provoke
discussion ; and he went on :

"The Gaelic-speaking Scotch are as children who will never be grown ; if they find themselves more at ease in the Gaelic, it is because that is a narrow and poor plot of speech, and its boundaries, which they everywhere feel, keep them firm on their legs."

At this point the old woman also turned, and fixed her strangely limpid gaze upon the speaker. Following in its wake as·it rested on the impatient figure, and the low square brow which certainly seemed to promise a narrow gauge of sympathy, it appeared to me that it might have been said of either of these two beings that they "looked but on a stool." There was no common medium of perception for natures so adverse, and it was curious to see that no permanent sense of the momentary trouble which had caused her to seek for its source had remained to old Susan after that seemingly ineffectual regard.

We had felt ourselves called upon to reprove the pedlar's mistimed strictures : the depth and tenderness of the Celtic mood, the poetry of the Celtic attitude towards nature, must be apparent to any but the wilfully or congenitally blind. Even in that remnant of voice which time had left to this old woman, there was a trace of the wild pathos to be heard in the wind in the weird hour after sunset, an echo of the melody, a touch of the grace of an elder, which was a younger day. Such as it seemed to us, we loved it better than jarring words, and we begged to be permitted to hear more.

After a little casting about and consultation, our call was again responded to ; the song, as if to fortify our favourable opinion, had more of poetry in it than the last, and the voice grew less quavering and more expressive as it proceeded :

> "And did ye say ye loed me weel?
>   Then, kind sir, ye maun marrie me ;
> For that I darena wear my snood
>   Aft brings the saut tear to my ee."

The character emblematical of maiden purity which attaches to the ribbon worn round the head is here alluded to, and the sameness of the theme with that of the song which had gone before reinforcing the argument of the pedlar, he was quick to seize the opportunity of delivering himself of the fag end of doctrine that had been left upon his hands.

"We have here what I say," he pursued with an impatient gesture ; "it is ever the same ; two notes like the cuckoo—two notes, and no more. Murder and plunder that stands for war, and love as this whereof the old lady is telling ;—war that is too bloody and cruel, and love that is too kind."

"Their songs are of what they have known," responded the German, "and it makes the secret of their charm. They sing of war as it was practised

among themselves, with its lawless cruelty and occasional generosity of heroism ; and they sing of love
in all its simpler aspects of passion and sentiment,
from the tender domestic affection which steals forth
in cradle-songs, to the overwhelming emotion which
is as the baptism of youth, and, at its best, the con-
secration of a life which is truly human. They have
war and love for their themes—love throughout its
whole gamut, from the tenderest self-devotion to the
most exacting jealousy ; and over and above these,
they have—what you leave wholly out of the count
—the fervour of their religious instinct, the abiding
sense of the unseen."

"Yes, as I tell to you," retorted the pedlar, "they
are children, they have their bogies. But for the
want of breadth, the *Einseitigkeit* in the imagination
of the Celt, look only to their naming of natural
objects—their mountains, for instance : here in Mull,
Ben Môr, big mountain ; in Perth, Ben Môr ; in
Sutherland, Ben Môr ; in Inverness, Ben Môr."

"Ye'll get the boots frae the ingle, Maisie, or if
they're no just dry by now, ye'll turn about a sprinklin'
of wood-ashes in their insides," said Miss Macorquodale.

The foot-gear here alluded to was not that on which
the generous heart of our hostess has been seen
to yield its pride, but a heavy, patched pair of high-

lows, taken from those damp feet of her Swiss guest, which were now ensconced in slippers belonging to her nephew, while his own shoes were slowly hardening at a distance from the fire.   In the present attitude of Miss Macorquodale there was something more than the wounded dignity of which I had early had experience ; she had clearly felt the discourtesy of the pedlar's strictures upon her people, and the tendering him his boots at this juncture was a suggestion, as imaginatively delicate as that conveyed in the action of that lovely bas-relief of a Victory unsandalling herself on alighting in conquering Athens.   The indirect intimation was the nearest approach, that our hospitable hostess was able to make, of a willingness to part with a guest from under a roof, which summer and winter had ever a bed ready for the reception of needy wayfarers.   It appeared highly probable that the hint was of too subtle a nature to take effect in the present instance, for the pedlar in lacing his shoes was preparing to resume the thread of his discourse, when a method occurred to me of at once showing my gratitude to Susan MacArthur, and effecting a diversion.

"Do you like to hear poetry," I asked, "as well as to recite it ?"

"Ye'll no get the chance o' hearing pothry the day; it's e'en gone the gait o' the dancing."

"The leddy will maybe say some at you hersel'," said Miss Macorquodale.

"Yes, I will say some if you will like to hear it."

"I would like it dearly; it wad tent me o' the old times."

I made a hasty dive among the not too well plenished stores of memory, and came out with something which commended itself by its simplicity, and its terseness—that little poem of Moore pronounced by Byron to be *multum in parvo*—

"Rich and rare were the gems she wore."

It was a very small thank-offering in kind to Susan MacArthur, but I was glad to note in the quick intelligence of the old woman's eyes, as she followed the change of voices from the lady to the knight, the appreciative pleasure with which it was accepted.

"It is a bonny song, but ye tell it like that? Is it that ye canna sing?"

"Yes, it is that I cannot sing; that is my misfortune."

It needed no more to bring my own true knight to the rescue.

"She cannot sing in that sense, but she makes music for others to sing."

"Ye dinna say that! Was the song she was saying the now a song of her ain makin'?"

" No, not that one."

" What for does she no say her ain ? "

" Ye have sung three songs for the leddy," suggested Miss Macorquodale ; " she has given you back but one—a little one, and none of her own. Maybe she wouldna think well to deny you if you asked for us all what we havena gained the right to ask for ourselves."

" I could but read you something," I said ; " I cannot remember my own verses ; and a true Scot, Highland or Lowland, would as lief listen to a written sermon as a read song."

" Na, na,' we would thank ye kindly ; we wad e'en take it as it wass given."

The request was embarrassing, and it grieved me that it should be so. Feeling so happy and at one with these simple people, it was matter of regret that so little of what I had been able to deliver myself of appeared likely to come within the range of their sympathy. I felt it as a rebuke, a species of condemnation. My deliverer was again at my side.

" Will you hear some little pieces such as she will give you herself, or shall I read to you all the longer poem she has just made on a thing that happened in this very Island of Mull—that took place yonder in the old Castle, and partly, perhaps, on the very spot where we are now gathered—the story that you all

know of the lady who was exposed on the rock out
there by the Maclean who was lord of the castle and
chief of the clan three hundred years ago "——

"We will hear the story of the Lady of the Rock!"
broke in several voices.

" It is too long," I urged.

" How long may it be ? " asked Miss Macorquodale.

" An hour," said the intending reader.

" An hour and a half," said I.

" Let it be two," pronounced Miss Macorquodale,
"and there will be time enough whatever between
this and the first dinner. The fire is made up, the
potatoes is peeled ready ; there will be nothing to
do but put the pie under the pot, and rake the ashes
over. Oh, it will be a beautiful time we shall have !"

The feeling of the little assembly was unanimous ;
there was a slight stir of preparation ; for old Susan
there was found an arm-chair near the fire, in place
of the seat on which she had hitherto been perched ;
Maisie made some rapid dives into mysterious regions,
from which she returned with an apronful of French
beans, and the pan of water wherein she was to throw
them in course of preparation ; Miss Macorquodale,
having installed me in what she meant to be the
place of honour, took up and began hastily to spear
her knitting ; and the pedlar, who having in vain
sought a hearing for a rather lengthy panegyric of

G

the brevity of " Rich and Rare," had risen to harness himself for the road, now quietly laid aside his pack and his tray, and gathered himself into his old critical attitude. Upon the scene thus prepared Helmuth returned with the manuscript, and to the intermittent accompaniment of the rising wind, the wash of the high-tide waves, and the click of Miss Macorquodale's needles, he began in a clear voice which lent music to the words :—

THE RHYME OF THE LADY OF THE ROCK.

FITTE THE FIRST.

Rose-red for the banner of love,
  And a blush for the cheek of the bride ;
To the valleys and hills of fair Loch Fyne
  The word went far and wide :
They will marry this day, and marry to death,
Our flower of ladies, Elizabeth.

On through the valleys and down from the hills,
  As the gathering cry of the clan
Had called them forth, through the moithering mist
  The lieges rode or ran
To meet at the foot of the runic cross,
And wring out the heart of their wrong and loss.

And there met them here and there on the breeze,
  Faint as a word of shame,
The sound of a bell, but they knew not well,
  As dubiously it came,
Or whether it chimed, or whether it tolled,
But they thought a knell had been more bold.

And they questioned the wind as it rose and fell
  Above and about Loch Fyne—
The wind that lashed at the shrinking wave,
  And harried the grove of pine—
Is your cry as the cry of her love on the rack,
Or only our lady's coronach?

But when they had come to the cross, and thence
  Peered over the castle wall,
And beheld the rout that was thronging the court,
  And the train that swarmed out of the hall—
With the banners that flaunted beside the door,
And the dog and the ship that the banners bore—

And saw by the fiery beard and eyes,
  And the motions cold and dull,
That the man who was leading the bartered bride
  Was Maclean of Duart in Mull,—
Then they knew they had married to worse than
    death
Their flower of ladies, Elizabeth.

Rose-red is the banner of love,
  But this bride is pale, snow-pale,
And she grows snow-cold as he helps her to horse,
  As the touch of the groom were bale;
But she proudly follows the lead of fate,
Nor once looks back when she passes the gate.

Some tuneless souls will meet, and make
   No answering music here,
But keep in our low, reverberate air,
   The peace of the outer sphere,
And passing, mix with the silent dead
And leave the word of our life unsaid.

But not Glenara's falls at "spate,"
   With their lusty voice for praise,
And not the vocal heart of spring
   That beats in its covert ways—
Not stream, or merle, or 'plaining dove
Went ever so near to utter love

As twain who under the "marriage-tree"
   Once heard their voices all,
And sent a confluent answer back
   To the cuckoo's double call,—
A sudden note so piercing sweet,
   It drowned the waterfall,—
Till with the primrose she grew pale,
He, wakeful with the nightingale.

For all as wise as their hearts had been
   To know and to claim their own,
They saw how oft by the felon world
   Love's dues are overthrown :

The world that knows not thine or mine,
But snatches a treasure from off a shrine.

And so it fell that the deep Argyle
 Had a bargain he would make,
And his sister must be the seal of it,
 Should it burn her heart or break.
Thus he married her to the slow, the dull,
Red-bearded tyrant, the chief of Mull.

The clansmen saw her where she came
 In the hold of the red Maclean,
Who once had ridden more free than free
 With love at her bridle-rein,
And passing left them for lingering trace
The smile that had flowered on every face.

They let her go with never a word—
 Was never a word to say ;
MacCallum Môr was lord of all,
 And his will must have its way ;
Though the heart of the speechless bride was
  wrath
As the torrent roaring beside her path.

But when to Cladich ferry they came,
 And the chief had called a halt,
While his shaggy train on bite and sup
 Were making swift assault,

She lighted down, and knelt beside
An image of the Crucified.

There, overborne with the stroke of fate,
   As droopingly she sunk,
She had not known how near her heart
   There knelt a cowlèd monk,
Till he took her hand and whispered low,
And she felt it riven with joy and woe.

Here was the voice in all the world,
   For her the only voice—
The hand whose touch in face of death
   Had made her sense rejoice;
And for these hearts with love so rife,
One moment but of common life!

"Up, love, and fly!" For one heart-beat
   Love had and held his own:
They mingled breath, they mingled tears—
   A word and he had flown,
Had carried her over ford and dyke
From Campbells and Macleans alike.

She strove with him, she clasped the cross:
   "Let pine," she said, "or die,
But never from this fore-front of fate
   Tempt me to fail or fly;

It has not been laid upon any man,
But on me to suffer and save the clan.

"MacCallum Môr has spared to meet
  Maclean as in open fight,
So awake or asleep in his island keep
  I must face him day or night;
For a true Argyle is but one thing sure:
The will and the word of MacCallum Môr."

They looked to right, they looked to left:
  O fair and cruel world!
Where tender firstlings of the spring
  On gusts of March are hurled,
The wild wind bent the pine-tops tall,
It rent the folded leaves, and small;—
The mocking sun laughed down on all.

They looked to left, they looked to right,
  And lo, through the cloven mist,
Loch Awe, that laughed to the laughing sun,
  As stormily they kissed.
"Cold sun," she said, "and bitter bliss,
Dear love, be witness: never kiss
Of man shall mar the print of this!"

A heavy freight bore down that day
  The Cladich ferry-boat,

And one that saw it had leifer seen
  It founder, I think, than float.
" Better a bride so foully wed
Were bedded here in the lake," he said.

But the lake would none of them, bride or groom,
  Or scurvy train, and tossed,
'Twixt Cladich ferry and Brander Pass,
  The boat that crossed and crossed ;
And the eyes that hung on the throat of the pass
Saw, blocking the way of love, the mass

Of dark Ben Cruachan, or ere they turned
  In wrath from the path of men ;
And the way-worn bride, by forest and flood,
  Through moss and reedy fen,
Went, forced on her way in the teeth of the wind
By the men of Mull who were trooping behind.

They cross the Sound ; the dim isle seems
  Adrift in the wind and rain,
As cold in the shadow of Castle Duart
  Its sodden shore they gain,
But the iron click of the stanchioned gate
Rings home like the closing jaws of Fate.

Her bower-maidens had busked the bride,
  The feast was long and loud,
But she scarce had sat at the board more still
  Had she sat there in her shroud.
And her courage failing for wearihead :
"'Tis a far cry to Loch Awe," she said.

"The end of the first Fitte," announced the reader, pausing and laying down the manuscript.

I thought the company a little straitened in their minds by the consciousness of the laudatory effusiveness which might be expected of them under the circumstances. Whether this was the case or not, I pass over expressions of approval which to my ear had no very genuine ring, though they were satisfactory as showing that the audience was yet wide awake, and in a mood to contribute a willing share to any spiriting the poem might bring to bear on it.

"It's a far cry to Loch Awe," repeated old Susan ; "that'll be the slogan o' the Clan Campbell ; poor leddy, a far cry, a far cry."

"Ah, she'll have fine to do between this and the end of her time at Duart," said Miss Macorquodale. "It's no sae pleasing for a man when his mind iss made up for one woman to have to take on wi' another ; but there iss more of the men-folk, I'm thinkin', than there iss of us—they are better able to halve themselves whatever. That leddy in the poem has a high spirit; she wadna stoop so low as the false Maclean without a fall that wad go nigh to shake the best of it out of her."

"You are right, Miss Macorquodale," I returned; "to stoop so low is to fall; but this lady was not made for that."

"Na," acceded Miss Macorquodale reflectively, "not without breaking."

"And nothing of her was broken," I said; "she was whole enough to hold her own against the elements unloosed in that night of terror upon the rock out there. Life, as it seems to me, must have had a high value for one who could make such a stand for its preservation. And here I must mention, that shortly after the reading had begun, a shadow had darkened the door which proved to be that of Archie Cumming, returned somewhat earlier than usual from his morning rounds of inspection, and hearing the measured cadence of the reading voice, he had paused upon the threshold, bent forward, and cast a sweeping glance around upon the various persons composing the listening group. Now the sound of rhythmic words was as the chime of the waves upon a shingly shore to the spirit of Archie Cumming, upon which their music laid a burthen of its own, independent of more direct, and often inadequately expressed meaning. A quiet look of pleasure stole into his dreamy glance, as doffing his Scotch bonnet and bending his head, he picked his way noiselessly across the floor, like one entering a church in the time of prayer, and leaning his back very quietly against the high chimney-piece, composed himself into an attitude of profound attention.

"It seems that the poem the gentleman is reading is of the story that we in these parts know best," he observed in his deliberate tones.

"Yes," said the reader, "it is the Rhyme of the Lady of the Rock, it has been composed here on the spot by "—— But I was at his side before he had got so far, knowing by experience that no sign short of actual contact, even to the extreme extent of a finger laid upon the lips, had 'ever been known to turn the tide of Helmuth's eloquence when in full flow upon such a theme.   In the present instance I was anxious not to forego the advantage of having one auditor at least whose interest in my work would be unhampered by any thought of my own authorship. As my back was to Mr. Cumming, and my person acting as a screen between him and Helmuth, the transference of this idea was in the present case not difficult.

"Is it the ballad of the great poet who bore the name of Campbell?" asked our host.

"No, it is the work, such as it is, of a woman, whose name as a poet will be unknown to you," I replied, at the same time making a sign to Miss Macorquodale, whose eyes, fixed on her unconscious nephew, expressed some natural anxiety about the reception of my poem on its own unassisted merits.

"I should like to remark," said Mr. Cumming in his low voice, "that the nightingale is a bird unknown to us in Scotland."

"Every child might inform you so much!" exclaimed the pedlar, whose impatient changes of position, as the word was taken by one or other of us, had caused the wooden chair beneath him to groan like a living creature unduly sat upon. "The common nightingale, *Philomela luscinia,* extends its migration on the continent of Europe as far north as Sweden, but in the British Isles no farther than Yorkshire. But what of that? An English poet who writes of the spring—the spring of the year, the spring of life—what you will—must have his '*decor*' of the season, his 'properties' to help him to conjure with. Bah! they are but false bottoms many of them, but—what would you?—they serve him for the trick."

I had not anticipated the turn that things had taken; to find myself championed by the critic as against the mild enthusiast was a surprise; but on the whole I felt little comforted by this transposition of parts.

"If the poet," I urged, "uses the nightingale as part of what you call the 'decoration' of the spring, he uses it not as a juggler or a cheat, he but takes it as a thing that he has known and believes in. If he carries it into regions where it is not, he must be convicted of ignorance, but not necessarily of insincerity."

"There are ancient songs of Scotland wherein the nightingale is made to sing," said Archie Cumming.

"The prime of the poets of the world would have cut a poor figure in a Natural History exam. before the last generation," returned the Swiss; "but it was all right if they could only keep up the game." He called it "gem," and his faulty pronunciation, together with his fluent use of slang, added unreasonably to my annoyance.

"You may count in a genuine Gaelic poem on the truth of its assertions," retorted Cumming, with an unwonted echo in his tone of the sententiousness of the Lowland Scot.

"And in all poems of the golden, as contrasted with the bookish ages," I put in.

"I am thinking," said the pedlar, looking past me to Cumming, "of greater men than ever spoke in Gaelic—your Spensers, and your Miltons, and

Popes. Where they wanted an object to make good the picture, they put it; they were bound by the laws of metre, and generally of poesie; but they were free-booters for any other. Nightingale, tender tale— something stale, I grant you that; what then? They fill up the pauses without breaking the spell."

I was feeling concerned for my couplet, having entertained a regard for it which now appeared to have been wholly beyond its desert, and I was already thinking how I might change what had been true for me to what could have been true for the Campbell cousins.

> "Till with the primrose she grew pale,
> He, wakeful with the nightingale."

"What bird is there other than the nightingale," I asked of Archie Cumming, "that makes its wakefulness known by song or cry, and whose name would rhyme with pale?"

"There is the land-rail," replied the farmer; "he is likewise a migrating bird, and the male arriving on these shores a fortnight before the female, may be heard in lonely places, keeping the night awake as you may say, with his short, dissatisfied cry."

"The night and those who have need to sleep therein," burst forth the pedlar with an injured air. "I made for myself the experience in a night of spring, lying on the sheltered side of a dyke not far

from this same Loch Fyne.   The land-rail is a weak,
tricky bird ; it will feign to be dead, thinking in that
way to escape your malice ; but it is easy taken in
with its own coin, for, like to deceivers in general, it
is not less but more to be bamboozled than others.
I laid myself flat like a dead weasel, and held in my
breath, when the fellow whose call had been the
sharpest came brushing my ear.   If his summons
was heard of a bride, it did not get him a wife ; I
put out my hand and took him—a bundle of feathers
with a little limp body inside—but warm, and with
a heart that you might count the beats of ; but for
that, he was a better actor than I.   Anyway he kept
me not from sleep the last half of that night."

I did not like the story, and while it was in progress had been trying to rearrange my peccant
couplet without altering the sentiment :

"Till with the primrose she grew pale,
   He, wakeful with the lone land-rail,"

I thought this awkward and dismissed it, when
Helmuth, who had been engaged in sorting the mixed
sheets of the manuscript, having now got them into
order, began in few words to recapitulate the leading
points of the narrative as laid down in the first Fitte.
He feared, and with some reason, that the discursive
turn the conversation had taken, might have disturbed the current of sympathy.

"In the first stanza," said he, "you will remember to have come upon the rumour of the sudden marriage, and in those immediately following to have seen the grief and dismay with which the tidings were entertained by the clan. After this we are shown that the upshot of this hasty marriage, with a man of evil nature, is doubly threatening, by reason of the bride's love and troth having been given to another. Where a halt has been called in the train that is bearing her to her doom, on the road above Cladich ferry, she meets her lover; and while resisting, in the interest of their common clan, his entreaties to evade her fate by flight, she swears to maintain herself pure, come what may, in the memory of the love of which she is taking leave. She has arrived at Mull, the gate of the castle has closed upon her, and she is seated at the feast which welcomes the married pair, when this first part of the poem ends. We will now resume "——

"Your pardon, sir," interrupted Archie Cumming, "but I should like, if so please you, before proceeding further, to hear the opening lines of the poem. They would serve me as a key, maybe, to the music of the rest, wherein there were certain lines that fell upon the ear as something strange."

    " Rose-red for the banner of love,
      And a blush for the cheek of the bride;

H

> To the valleys and hills of fair Loch Fyne
>   The word went far and wide :
> They will marry this day, and marry to death,
> Our flower of ladies, Elizabeth."

"Rose-red for the banner of love," struck in the strange pedlar, his soiled left hand outstretched and telling off the beats of the verse upon its thumb and fingers with the index of his right; "opens with a spondee, trips off into anapests; confusion of anapests and iambics in the third line; iambics pure in the fourth; confusion worse confounded, as you say, in the fifth and sixth !" And the learned itinerant merchant, having spread his two arms abroad and shrugged his shoulders without taking them down again, turned an accusing look upon me as the author of all this anarchy.

I am loth to fight, whatever may be the call, but there are occasions on which you cannot decline the party with honour; and I felt this to be one. Helmuth looked at me, Archie Cumming looked at me—the one glance expectant, the other inquiring; Miss Macorquodale looked at the critical pedlar with a fixity of scorn which might have perturbed a more sensitive spirit.

"The author of these lines," I said, for I still retained enough of presence of mind to guard my part in them from Mr. Cumming, "has taken for

Pegasus a Highland sheltie, believing its paces better suited to the rough ground to be gone over, than those of a higher bred courser. In the heat of progress she has not measured the length of the stride, but it has been subject to law of which I believe the rule could in every case be found, if honestly sought for; where rapid action or variety of objects has to be suggested, there of themselves break in the anapests; the iambics give the more sustained movement, the spread as of a wave, as in ‘The word went far and wide’.”——

“Your Highland sheltie is known for a clever beast,” said the Swiss, “but he must be very what you call ‘canny’ indeed if that he can suit his action to the word in such manner as you have presented him with the power, madam; and even then, a horse that is good for anything, be he pad or racer, breaks not out of a trot to a gallop, but preserves an even pace”——

“Till touched with the hand or spur,” I broke in; “but the air of the Highlands is keen, and Highland blood is hot, and easily stung into motion. In choosing her rough Pegasus, the lady has had confidence in his natural cunning—she has not felt it to be calculation—and has been careful only that he should do his work in the midst of his own surroundings. She gave him his head when he felt himself at home, let him creep down the side of a rock like a cat, or climb it as he thought best ; suffered him to feel with a hoof, as sensitive as a hand, for the safe places in the bed of a stream, and change his pace as it suited the nature of the ground to be got over.   But we had best continue the reading," I resumed, sensible that my mood was becoming too lyrical for the advancement of truth ; "the picture will else get lost in the frame."

"Enough of the commentary, let us return to the text," said Helmuth ; "I find no fault with the paces."

"And the gentleman," asserted Archie Cumming with his quiet smile, "would be the first to feel it ; he could not keep his seat so steady if the nag you speak of changed his feet without due warrant."

"The gentleman is a good rider," said the pedlar, "and he favours, and knows how to favour, his beast."   But the compliment was coldly received.

"Remember," said the bepraised cavalier with some show of impatience, "that the lady and her attendants have been conveyed over the sea to Mull, and that we left her before all this irrelevant talk, sitting silent at the loud feast which was in progress, here, close by us, in Castle Duart."   And he pointed over his shoulder in the direction of the old tower, as if the wassail had been going forward at the moment.

Upon this the party settled themselves, and the reading was resumed.

FITTE THE SECOND.

THE wassail had reached its stormy height,
  The feast was over in hall,
When there came and stood at the lady's side
  A gloomy seneschal;
As he pointed the way to a turret near
She knew that it led to the bride chambère.

And she that was rose of fair Argyle—
  A white rose she was then !—
Stood up and waited no second sign,
  But bowed to the roystering men,
And passed with her bower-maids out of the hall
I' the lead of the wordless seneschal.

Then some who noted her proud and pale
  Bent laughing over the board:
"She is white as a widow's callant," they said,
  "Who should whet a maiden-sword."
And in sooth the Lady Elizabeth
Had blithelier followed the feet of Death
Than the form which, fronting the torch's glare,
Cast a giant shade on the turret stair.

And when she stood in her bridal bower,
  She turned to her maidens twain :
"No hand but this of mine may dress
  The bride of the red Maclean ;
So lend me but your prayers this night,
And fare ye well till the fair daylight."

She cast her garments one by one,
  Alone as she stood there ;
She was to sight no summer flower
  But a woman deadly fair,
When forth she drew the golden comb
  And loosed the golden hair
Which sheathed her body to her knee,—
A ringed and burnished panoply.

Then, as a swimmer, with her arms
  The amber flood she spurned
To either side, and in her hand
  She took a gem that burned—
That rose and fell upon her heart
As a thing that bore in its life a part.

'Twas a golden dragon in jewelled mail
  That lay betwixt breast and breast
Over that gentle lady's heart,
  Couched as a lance in rest ;

And that cunning sample of goldsmith's work,
It was the handle of a dirk.

She drew it forth of its leathern sheath,
  And she felt its steely edge,
Then gave some drops of her quick young blood
  To its point, as if in pledge,
Ere she wound her hair in a silken thong,
And the dirk in that golden chain and strong.

She laid the dragon again to sleep
  In its balmy place of rest :
O God, that a home so soft and fair
  Should harbour such a guest!
Then her winsome self she re-arrayed,
And fell on her trembling knees and prayed.

She muttered many an Ave then,
  And told off many a bead,
Till her passion sealed her lips, for words
  But mocked so sore a need;
Then she stopped and listened beside the breeze,
And only waited upon her knees.

And as she listened, the distant sound
  Of wassail ceased, and all
Her soul rushed armed into her ears
  At sound of a dull foot-fall

Which wound its way to the topmost tower
Where was the lady's bridal bower.

The wind was piping through lock and loop,
    But of nothing was she 'ware,
There was no sound in all the world
    But that foot upon the stair ;—
And as she listened, and heard it rise,
Her soul rushed armed into her eyes.

She stood up white in her snowy pall,
    A breathing image of death,
The torch-light crowning her radiant hair,
    Her sombre face beneath.
" As I am a virgin pure this night,
So keep me, God, through dark to light ;
As I am a child of the deep Argyle,
Souls of my fathers ! teach me wile."

The iron door on its hinges turned
    And closed on the married twain,
And redder yet from his deep carouse
    There stood the red Maclean ;
And their four eyes met, and no word was said
Till his glance fell off on the vacant bed.

Then she : " I have prayed of Mary's grace
    That she would us assoil

For that this day with lips forsworn
  We sought to cut the coil
Of mortal hate that has ever lain
Betwixt the Argyle and Maclean."

Then low he laughed : "To kneel and pray,
  Lady, beseemeth thee,
But to make of our false oath a true
  Is the task that fitteth me ;
My word, before the morrow's sun,
You shall avouch the work well done."

He moved a step to where she stood,
  And she recoiled a pace ;
His wandering eyes again were set
  In wonder on her face.
They paused, they made a mutual stand ;
His breath fell hot upon her hand.

"You are a lord of the Isles," quoth she,
  "And the Islemen's mood is light,
But I am a child of the firm mainland,
  And I change not in a night.
There is nought of me that a man may win,
And I think not to overlay sin with sin.

"Now nothing could hap that would make us twain
  But false as woman and man,

Yet by grace of God we may still be true
   Each to our name and clan,
And each to each in a sidelong way
True to the bond we have sealed this day.

" You asked for a gage of my feudal chief,
   But of me nor word nor smile ;
You sought but to better the strength you had
   With the strength of the deep Argyle ;
You shall have your due and no more of me
Than a contract's seal and warrantry."

He laughed in his beard : " Ay, many have tried,
   But all have tried in vain,
To mete with a measure that was not his
   The due of the red Maclean ;
Still with iron hand he has held his right,
But never so close as he will this night."

She set herself as a hind at bay,
   She straightened her back to the wall ;
" I that am come as a hostage here,
   Would you use me as a thrall ? "
" Not so," quoth he, " but by limb and life,
I'll use you as my wedded wife."

" I am an earl's daughter," she said,
   " And my oath is worth a knight's,

And I swear by the health of my mother's soul,
 That the kiss which first alights
On me as we two lie in bed,
Shall have the force to strike me dead."

" You are an earl's daughter," he said,
 " And a maid without a stain ;
But as you are here in Castle Duart,
 And I am the red Maclean,
That oath shall no more be your screen
Than if you were the veriest quean."

She shrunk as into the granite wall,
 She parried his rude embrace ;
His fierce eyes glowed like the autumn fern,
 His breath was hot on her face ;
Her heart seemed knocking against the stone,
It beat as it would burst her zone.

She cried a cry, but it fell still-born,
 It died in her throat for fear,
Though the meaning ablaze in the dauntless
  gaze
 Of her flame-blue eyes was clear ;
And it was that the Lady Elizabeth
Was ready to give as to take of death.

Her hand bore hard on her heaving breast,
  And he knew whereto it clung,
And saw how her eyes on the turn of his,
  Two deadly warders, hung;
Then his caitiff soul succumbed to hers,
  He let her go, and sprung
Back with the cry of a ravening beast
Baulked on the eve of a gory feast.

Twice already that tyrant chief
  Had seen th' accusing steel
Cleaving the way to his savage heart
  In a victim's last appeal;
And he hated more the better he knew
The flash of that lightning cold and blue.

He glanced at the dagger's golden string,
  And his sodden wit grew clear;
"Wear to, wear to, I will stalk this maid,
  As we stalk the Highland deer."
The fumes of wassail that left his brain
  Had left it free to fear;
"She is yet too wild," he said, "and deep
To be taken waking or asleep."

He spoke her fair: "You have journeyed far,
  By mountain and by flood,

And to you of all that life hath dear,
  Sleep only seemeth good;
So you shall taste untroubled rest
This night as 'twere a stranger guest."

Her left hand sheathed the shining dirk,
  She gave to him her right :
"Now lay your sword betwixt us two
  As you are a belted knight.
Then God be watch and ward," she said,
And stretched herself by the sword in bed.

And hourly, as the night wore on,
  She lay in the deepening gloom,
Her two hands folded upon her breast
  Like a statue on a tomb ;
But she seemed to feel the dirk beneath
Her fingers tingling in its sheath.

And the moon came softly out of a cloud
  I' the midmost of the night,
And through the loop-hole gazed at her,
  She lying still and white
Beside the castle's lord, who slept
While she her wary vigil kept.

But when the morning's face rose pale
  O'er the shoulder of Cruachan-ben,

She stole from out the bride chambère,
  A joyful woman then ;
And alone in face of the risen sun
She dared to weep : the day was won !

"End of the second Fitte," said Helmuth ; and no
words followed for a minute or two.   I liked this
silence better than the somewhat perfunctory notes of
admiration which had greeted the conclusion of the first
part. It was clear that these several persons, gathered
together in a remote spot, far from the solicitings of
all counter-excitement, and with imaginations stimulated by the near neighbourhood of the scene in
which the persons of the drama had lived, were completely under the spell.   That this was so, had been
evident from their various attitudes of attention as the
narrative advanced ; in the suppressed exclamations
of Miss Macorquodale ; the involuntary mouthings of
the old woman ; the absorption, at once hushed and
eager, of Mr. Cumming ; and in a less degree, in the
cessation of the restless movements by which the
hawker was wont to mark off the points to which
his keen wit had taken exception.   Maisie for her
part had let fall her hand with the knife in it, upon
the side of the vessel, wherein she ceased to drop the
beans, and her eyes looked darker from—yes, there

could be no mistake—from the ebbing of the rich
young blood which usually flushed her cheek. She
resumed, and hastily completing her operations,
bestirred herself about the fire before gathering together on the side of the dresser some objects to
which friction might be supposed to be profitable,
and which would in any case give a countenance to
her presence when the reading should be again in
progress. Helmuth had felt these signs, and others
still more impalpable, in the air, and it had given
a more stirring vibration to his voice. For me, I
gathered them I know not how, for certainly of
all who were moved by the images called up, none
were so little cool or apt for critical observation as
myself. The kitchen of Miss Macorquodale seemed
quite to have disappeared, and, the occasional wail of
the constantly rising tempest aiding, to have rendered
its place to that tower chamber not a furlong off,
where " the wind was piping through lock and loop,"
and the stand for dear love had been made.

But the pedlar was not going to succumb to the
influences of time and place, or the infection of primitive feeling, without a protest, and the occasion of a
natural reaction was not far to seek.

" Your lady has set her pen to work on a perilous
subject as addressed to your 'Philister' English
public," said he.

My visions were scattered in a moment; like a jewelled window through which a bullet has passed, the hues of fancy grew dark and dull with the inlet of common day. I involuntarily looked at Maisie. I had seen the ordinarily shy eyes uplifted, and marked the fair self-forgetful face as she listened to the brave words of Elizabeth Campbell, with no feeling that such were unmeet for the ear of a clear-souled girl, belonging to a world where innocence is not held to imply an ignorance of the conditions of virtue. I had faith in poetic truth, and no fear of simple nature, but I rather shrunk from the prose commentary upon them, and for the first time wished Maisie out of ear-shot, feeding the pigs with the beanstalks and the potato peelings.

"The danger you speak of is beneath contempt," said Helmuth; "there is no work here for the literary scavenger but such as he may make for himself."

"All the same I can make me a picture," returned the irrepressible pedlar, "of paragraphs in certain of your public prints wherein the critics will exalt themselves upon moral stilts, and will come down on "———

"Let them come," cried my champion, "let them lay about them with their wooden legs! They will overthrow nothing that is pure and true; the wounds they can make are not mortal; they can only harm what they can bring low. Let them come."

It was evident that he saw the rough handling, or rather footing, which the pedlar predicted for me as an experience, of which it was possible for him to receive the whole brunt; he would not otherwise have made so light of it. For my own part, I was now looking back upon the scene, and beholding it in the crude light which had entered at the hole made in it by the pedlar; I was conscious of the danger, and was troubled, and wishing that some choice of motive had been offered to me. To cover my discomfort I rose and turned towards the fire.

"She was a brave leddy," quavered old Susan, looking up with those eyes that were so pathetic in their sad surroundings, "eh, eh! a brave leddy, but there's many the like of her in the old songs."

"Yes, in the old songs. We love them and the people in them because they dared to be true, and because there was time in those days for the feelings to root themselves deeply."

I was talking to hide my annoyance, but through all I was able to observe, that the menacing expression which had drawn down Miss Macorquodale's long upper lip, appeared even to extend itself to the tongs which quivered in her hand, as she arose from trimming the fire, and faced the guest whom

I

she was beginning to regard from the unwonted
point of view of an intruder. A long look as of
a puzzled child had also fallen upon the same in-
vulnerable person from the soft eyes of Maisie,
while Mr. Cumming, still with that air of being in
church, which he had assumed on entering the kitchen,
was repelling extraneous objects from at least one
avenue of sense, with his hand before his eyes. The
discussion between Helmuth and the hawker was
still in progress, having run on counter to the
words of old Susan and myself like the opposing
voices of a fugue. It was Helmuth who was now
speaking.

"I am a German," he said, "but I have faith in
the candour of Englishmen. The heroic temper of
that whole scene in the tower chamber must, will be
felt to, lift it aloft, clear out of reach of the imputa-
tions you suggest. Outspoken it is, as it should be,
but the voice that utters itself is from the purest as
from the strongest heart of womanhood "——

"Be it so," broke in the pedlar, grimly smiling as
he threw himself back, making the chair groan, and
leaving tokens of his mud-encrusted boots upon Miss
Macorquodale's floor; "'Be thou pure as ice,' as
says your Hamlet, 'you shall not escape calumny.'
The ladies who choose to forsake the covered ways
and to 'walk in the sun,' must take the chances that

will befall them. You will be there with your umbrella, but will it help?"

The pedlar was perhaps right, there was trouble in
the wind; but whoever aspires to wings must be free,
free of the air, free of the sun; on no other condition
can the art cultivated be robust or even sane. I had
written of what, as a woman, I could feel as possibly
no man could; if there was toll to pay in taking that
path, I would pay it, bringing this small sacrifice
to the cause of freedom, as many a woman in this
generation has brought a greater. I looked up clear,
ashamed of my momentary cowardice.

"If the gentleman would kindly read on," suggested Mr. Cumming. We were all in our several
ways relieved by this proposition, and a temporary
lull having taken place in the weather without, a
silence was made for the reader's voice, only broken
by the occasional ebullition of an iron pot, which
caused some uneasy wandering in the thoughts of
Miss Macorquodale.

FITTE THE THIRD.

WHEN the morning board with the rests of the feast
    Was set, and the martial kin—
The vassals in chief of the castle's lord—
    Still heavy with sleep dropped in,

They found a smiling chatelaine
Threading her keys on a silver chain.

And still when her lord, like a thunder-cloud
  Full-charged, came louring down,
With her own white hand she served to him
  The prime of the venison ;
So tending him in the downward eyes,
It 'hoved him nor to speak or rise.

Thus every morning she was meek
  As a loving wife might be,
And full of service and soothfastness
  As a lady of high degree :
In house and hall a guiding power,
A gracious presence in lady's bower.

At eventide she graced the feast
  With a face of merry cheer,
And her voice to the harp when the harp went
    round,
  As the laverock's note was clear :
So " she singeth in the night, they say,
As a bird that singeth in the day."

And seeing her so amenable
  And lovely in daylight hour,

Her lord would follow as time might serve
   For dalliance in lady's bower,
Where sitting apart on the window stone
They parleyed together as if alone.

And once, she making the shuttle fly,
   Her maidens spinning near,
He seized her fluttering hands, and laughed :
   "They are captives, white with fear."
"Nay, call them rather," she laughed back,
"Pale victims, faithful on the rack."

And seeing her frail, as she was fair,
   He measured with thievish eye
The length of the dirk which clove her breast,
   And thought where the hilt might lie ;
But he saw no way through her silken suit,
Which clipt her close as the rind the fruit.

And seeing her fair, as she was frail,
   In the sting of a new-born need,
His tuneless voice for once rang true,
   His fierce tongue learnt to plead.
Then her daylight face was in eclipse,
The shadow of night on her eyes and lips,

As she answered him : "While the stars endure
   You will get no more of me

Than what you hold at my brother's hand,
    For a gift is of the free :
That hour which made us two handfast,
The time to win as to woo, was past."

"You are haggard, dame, as a hawk," he said,
    As he gave her hands reprieve,
"But we tame the wildest tercelet
    That ever we let live."
Then he rose and left the bower in wrath,
And the stones cried out upon his path.

"Craft is the strength of Argyle ; she knows
    Our heads are under one hood,
But that hood shall be cover for mine alone,
    If ever meseemeth good ;
The sleuth-hound in vain, if he failed of that,
Had been held in leash with the mountain cat.

"*Now* is better than *then ;* good brother Argyle,
    New love is like new wine ;
I will put to the proof this brotherly shield,
    Before it is worn too fine,
And see when my hand has done a thing,
How you make it good in the eye of the king."

He called aloud to his namesmen all,
    As they loitered about the court ;

"Come, rouse ye, men, for a bloody raid,
   And I warrant ye good sport ;
The better that we by night shall stoop,
And seize our prey in a silent swoop.

"And some of your band must go by land,
   And some shall come by sea ;
And those shall ride with Malcolm Môr,
   And these shall sail with me ;
Our meeting-place Glengarry Bay :
The boats, there needs no more to say."

Then some to horse, and some to ship,
   Some sailed, some rode or ran ;
While shrill at their head the pipers played
   The gathering of the clan ;
The work was death, the road was rough,
They knew no more, it was enough.

But when they came to Loch-na-kiel,
   Nor pipe nor voice was heard,
You might have caught, as you brushed the ling,
   The cry of a brooding bird,
And a league or ever you reached the shore,
Have steered by the dull Atlantic roar.

Then warily they at Glengarry Bay
   Make sign to the waiting boat,

And the word goes round whereto they are bound,
    As they silently get afloat;
And they steal upon Cairnburg's island keep,
Where it lies in the cradling surf asleep.

Then little they heard of the scared sea-bird
    Or the near Atlantic roar,
For the fierce war-clang of the crossing swords
    As led by Malcolm Môr.
They stormed the keep, and its keepers slew,
    Or laid in irons before;
Maclean with his merry men sailed in,
Safe to conquer, and bold to win.

He passed the body of Cairnburg's lord
    With its gaping wounds and red,
And he spurned it from him with his foot—
    He did not fear the dead;
Then he filled a horn and gave a toast,
"We'll drink," quoth he, "to our silent host."

The thirsty crews swarmed up, they left
    The dead men and the bound,
And, drunk with blood, in wassail deep
    Their reeling senses drowned.
The captive's groans, the victor's glee,
The lashing of the ruthless sea,
Made up the wild world's harmony.

O loving God, whom all men loved
  When hating most their kind,
They lifted bloody hands in prayer,
  Now all are stricken blind,—
And we never more may see the sun
Till all men's eyes and hearts are one !

The red Maclean set his signet seal
  On the castle's garnered store,
Then he filled his pouch with its gold, and gave
  The keys to Malcolm Môr,
Whom he left in charge, bold man and true,
While himself took ship with his jolly crew.

And he thought: "To this frost-bound maid of
    mine
  When I come red-handed in,
Will the ice of her virgin pride break up,
  Shall I come as I came, to win ? "
But the spirits that wrought for him by day
Were nought at night ; and she held her way.

Then he fell in longing by day and night
  As the sick man longs for health ;
And he longed for her by night and day
  As the beggar longs for wealth,
As one who hung over the pit of hell
Might clutch at a star-beam ere he fell.

And his stricken thought turned round on
    himself,
  And his dim low-lying soul
Caught a shadowy glimpse of a fairer way,
  As he deemed, to a fairer goal ;
So a heavier stone on his heart was flung,
Which helped but to sink him where he hung.

He dreamed of tortures of rare device
  As to give his passion ease,
And once in his dire extremity
  He sued her upon his knees ;
But alone, without her Campbell shield,
Who knows to die, needs not to yield.

For bulwark and for last defence
  She had the strength of steel :
The sword betwixt them was a sign,
  The dagger was a seal ;
And each fine hair that wound about
The dagger's hilt, a watchful scout.

But sitting alone on the window stone,
  Though still was the summer air,
She heard a whispering on the sea,
  A moaning she knew not where ;

Then she looked to the hills where the two
    winds meet,
And saw them wrestle together, and beat
Each against each, and pant and smoke
Like beasts that fret in unequal yoke.

And she said : "O love that I knew so fair,
    Whoever had thought of thee
That thy summery breath could raise the storm;
    And the wreck—whose shall it be?
Were the end but death, would it now were here,
And a white fringed pall on my maiden bier."

     "She heard a whispering on the sea,
      A moaning she knew not where,"

repeated Archie Cumming in welcome prolongation
of the sentiment. The whispering and moaning
peculiar to the place were familiar phenomena to
him as has been seen.

"Of this last that you have given us," said the
learned hawker, addressing Helmuth, "I can tell
you it is "—— and he shook his head and made a
gesture signifying that it was nought. "It is not
good enough, or it is too good. A book, prose or
verse, if it have not wit in itself, must as your poet
says, be the cause of wit in others ; we are getting

used to the untaught paces of your lady's Highland sheltie, we are no longer "——

"If the beautiful poem gives this gentleman no more to say," interrupted Miss Macorquodale, "it is the better for those that would like to be hearing it speak for itself."

Upon this hint Helmuth gathered up the manuscript, and fluttering its pages for a second or two as if to clear the air of adverse influence, resumed as follows :

FITTE THE FOURTH.

As the red Maclean went to and fro
   'Twixt Duart and Cairnburg tower,
One day he chanced to spy a rose ;
   It seemed a single flower
With an open eye, but in some close part
The bud was shaping a double heart.

And this flower grew up so fresh and fair
   On land that was held in fief,
The Treshnish Isles, which her father owned
   Of Maclean, a vassal chief,
And this fair maid, having a vassal soul,
Of her beauty paid the tyrant toll.

And his gallèd spirit found ease in her
  From the bond of the proud Argyle,
And his famished pride rose up full-fed,
  And rampant beneath her smile,
That he laughed his laugh : " I will take this flower
And plant as a thorn in my lady's bower."

So he took the maiden with him in croup,
  And to Castle Duart they came,
Where my lady looked her through and through,
  Without or pity or blame :
"Would God," she thought, "this flower would
    twine
And stablish herself in this place of mine ! "

So she let it be, and it wound and wound,
  It was so soft and young,
So lithe as the green shoots felt their way,
  But they hardened where they clung,
Till they bent the stake the way they chose ;
For this plant it was a climbing rose.

And the red Maclean, the chief of the clan,
  To her was the chief of men,
And she thought in her pride, " Could I win to his
    side,
  As the mists upon Cruachan-ben,

My matron coif would be borne so high
It would shine the first in the great world's eye."

Now Maclean in the strength of others is waxed
   So proud that nought avails,
But the ships that traverse the Sound of Mull
   Must lower their topmost sails,
When of Duart they come within gun-shot—
Still the woman who called him lord, bent not.

She looked from the seeming single flower
   That twined until, none knew how,
The tender shoot that had clasped a twig,
   Had all but bent a bough,
To her baffled lord, for his changed desire
Had held her safe in its counter-fire.

And he who noted her morning face
   Grow clearer and yet more clear,
Beheld her the only untamed thing
   Of all that came him near ;
And his longing was as the thirst for blood,
   His hate was the hate of fear ;
And the fear and longing so grew and grew,
That together they rove his heart in two.

And still he saw her the bond that bound
   Clan Campbell to his name,

And knew the issue between them, one
  That for very pride and shame,
In his strong walls filled with his vassal kin,
His hand unholpen must lose or win.

The round world spinning about the sun
  Appeareth a two-fold arc;
It nothing knoweth of high or low,
  But only of light and dark:
That many, dreaming they climb a height,
Are boring deep in the pitchy night.

So the wilding rose it crept and crept,
  It was so soft and fair,
That it wound till it reached the chamber door
  At the top of the turret stair;
As its sweetness weighted the air within,
She thought, "One night he will tirl the pin.

"He will open and put my lady forth,
  And will set me by his side."
And so it fell; and my lady rose
  And past in her virgin pride
From out of the chamber adown the stair
With a foot as light as a bird o' the air.

Then the fierce Maclean, when as chatelaine
  She greeted him from her place,
And he caught the tenser tone of her voice,
  The light on her morning face,
Was hounded as by the devils in hell
To quench the spirit he could not quell.

And his limmer, striking deeper root,
  Still darkly wound her way,
For she hated, who only reigned at night,
  The woman who ruled by day ;
And at Castle Duart the fiends full fain
Went up and down betwixt these twain.

Then the limmer made an image of wax,
  Alike in every part
To my lady's self, and when all was done,
  She stuck it through the heart :
" Dwindle and dwine in shade and shine,"
She said, " till all of thine be mine."

And ever beside the waxen shape
  In the gloaming of the day,
With folded hands she crooned the curse
  As a troubled soul might pray :
" Dwindle and dwine in shade and shine,
Till all be mine that now is thine."

In an evil hour the baffled chief
    Looked in as she crooned the spell;
He plucked the shroud from the waxen shape:
    " You have wrought this passing well;
My lady's face, and the smile thereof;
Here hate hath done the work of love.

" My lady's face as she lives——not so ;
    My lady's face," he said,
" Not as she lives to flout us two,
    But as——*she might lie dead.*"
Then each glanced up as in vague surprise,
And shrunk at the light in the other's eyes.

For the wish that was quick in the woman's breast
    Had mothered the thought of the man,
And he said : " Ay, harry this heart of wax,
    And the woman you would ban
Shall feel the sting in her heart of stone."
But his laugh rang hollow, and died a groan.

He seized the knife, he struck it anew
    And turned in the wounded wax :
" Take heed of this bloodless beauty," he said,
    "That thereof nothing lacks ;
We will keep this saint as in a shrine ;
She may be worth your life and mine."

He led his limmer forth, and turned
　The key ere he went his gait:
"If hate can do the work of love,
　So love the work of hate."
Then his fierce heart surged in its beaten pride
As the great waves surged in the high spring-tide.

　　This fourth canto, if not longer than the foregoing,
had seemed to me to drag a little, for in many places
during the reading of the latter part of it, had
Helmuth had to overcome the dissentient comments
of its foreign auditor, by raising his voice to a pitch
which effectually dominated the feebler organ of the
pedlar.

　　But, indeed, had there been no such interruption
calling for repression within our immediate circle,
the hurly-burly of the elements without would have
necessitated increased resonance in the voice which
aspired to make itself a solo with so wild an accompaniment.　There was a sound at whiles in the
chimney as of a flapping sail; the sleet in passing
would turn aside, and strike the window as with a
sudden blow; and the sea seemed almost upon us.
It was as if the spirit of the wind, which for a time
had left the place in peace, had returned with seven
others more turbulent than itself.　Yet no sooner

had the leading voice in the symphony subsided, than that of the Swiss hawker rushed in, made still more harsh and strongly gutteral in the effort to secure a hearing.

"This metrical story that you have been at the trouble to read us so far—it is well laid out; like the pieces in a child's puzzle, the parts fit into their places; like a child who builds his palace with toy bricks, the little touches are set one upon another"——

"Why like a child and not a man?" shouted Helmuth above the storm; "his procedure when he builds is precisely similar."

"True," cried the pedlar, "but the great artist does not build, he makes his thought visible in a stroke as of his wand. The ladies—it is the same with them all—are tied down to time, to time and to space; their sphere is *here*, and *now;* let them try to emancipate themselves from us others as they will, they may cast themselves from a height, but they will never follow us into the clouds."

"Pending further proof, that contention had best stand over," I exclaimed, "and in the meanwhile I demur to being taken into the count of what women, better endowed, and better equipped for the contest, may be able to achieve in the future." But nobody heard me.

"Of what women *cannot* do, *mein freund,*" in-

sisted the German, having recourse in his eagerness
to the native tongue, " we have heard and are hearing
too much ; the theme is trite, and is utterly unfruit-
ful. They have voices of different quality from ours
—voices for singing no less than for speaking, as
a woman has well pointed out, and the chorus of
humanity must for ever be incomplete without them.
Their tones you will say have less volume than ours ;
be it so. Is it fair to put our partition before them,
and contemn them that it is out of their compass ?
Are there no notes that they can touch, think you,
that are beyond our reach ? In the ultimate harmony
we want some sounds that are delicate and acute,
and we want them not manly but womanly ; it has
been found that such voices will ' carry ' far. Let
the wise ones seek in woman's work for the note of
woman's power ; could the critics find out and hold
up to the light some one thing, however small, that
singing women have nature's charter to utter more
fully than man, they would do knightly service in
the cause of music ; but they follow each other with
no more variety in their cry than the howling of
wolves in a pack."

" There is no such thing," shouted the Swiss, "as
women can do better than men. They have been
beaten along the whole line, and will be beaten at
every point."

"I say they are not beaten," persisted Helmuth, his blood by this time being fairly up; "the trial has never been made. Poetry—bah!—great poetry is rarer than the flower of the aloe, and it needs rare conditions to bring it to the birth. Among these is an atmosphere of welcome and expectation. Did such exist for the woman-poet a hundred years ago? Does it exist at this moment? And if it does —a few years, what are they to such an issue? How long was England waiting for her Chaucer? When she got him, how soon did Spenser follow?"

The pedlar made mien to answer, but the fight had become a scrimmage and the German was uppermost.

"I will not touch upon the greatest of all," he pursued, "unless to say that of all the men who ever wrote of women, he seems to be the only one who knew them distinctively, as a shepherd knows his sheep. For the rest they have generally been feature-less creatures, their very shapes lost in conventional fleeces—only ticketted harmless or dangerous accor-ding to the service required of them."

"And do the women fare better at each other's hands?" bawled the Swiss; "they get the last word as against us, but that is no new thing; do they prove themselves "——

"No more the last word than the Lady Macbeths, and the Beatrices, the Rosalinds, and the Imogens of the only man who has ever gone near to sounding their depth."

"Will you tell me "—— began the pedlar.

"I will tell you," exclaimed the other, availing himself of his stronger voice, for he felt justified in holding his ground by every means in contest with so adroit an adversary—"I will tell you that if the moral standard of the race is lower than it should be at this time of day, and lower for men than for women, it is to women that we must look to raise it. Who among men have done most to this end? The poets. It is by the travail of the poets of all ages that the conscience of humanity has been formed. They have done nobly, but they have not done all. We want women-poets to lend a hand to the work. The man's idea of woman is of a creature who makes life easy; one whose knees are prompt to bend in unmotived adoration, who is complaisant to a point which in men is deemed infamy. We want to keep some corner wherein to have our faults condoned. It is hard if the liar and the hypocrite cannot find an unquestioning receiver for his stolen goods in the wife of his bosom. The outside world is severely just; we would have our women to keep at home, out of the sun, out of the light, and the knowledge that must tell against ourselves. It is easier to darken the window than to clean the house."

"Bah! women will still be women," cried the pedlar, placing a thumb in each of his waistcoat pockets after drawing his fingers through his wisp of hair; "they are like this Celtic people that we are wandering amongst,—they have the instinct of worship." He offered a humorous picture in this attitude, but his interlocutor was too gravely in earnest to take delight in it.

"Our conceit would have it so," he thundered, "but the facts deny it. It is the senses that hood-wink the reason, and our senses are more rampant than theirs. The high-hearted woman with a clear ideal of conduct is a formidable critic of those in whom her pride is vested. The man who is cur enough to pine for the ignoble worship which brings down true hearts to the dust, had best go at once to Cathay;—it is only the belated and feeble spirits among the women of our time who will give it to him here. Tenderness, devotion, loyalty, yes: of that we shall find an ever-increasing quantity; but fret against it as we may, depend upon it, my friend, the best love of the best women has more in it of divine charity than is flattering to our self-love. They have a passion that we scarcely share : the passion of maternity ; the love that can strike them blind, is the love of children ; and even in that there is reason, for children belong to the future, and for the future there is always hope."

" If your lady is to be of the women-poets who point us out the way," said the pedlar, his voice all the more grating for a touch of sarcasm, " it would be well that she should show us charity through the persons of her creation, and not keep it all for private use, however needy the subject of it may be. The lawful wife of the chief in this story that has no hero, having taken unfair advantage of his natural infirmity —his want of what you call pluck—to defraud him of his due, is no model of Christian charity when she welcomes, and as you may say invites to sin, a maiden as for aught she knows who has done her no wrong, in the hope to spare her own daintiness. The eyes that can look on such a young girl without either pity or blame are cold eyes, and have little sense of what belongs to "——

" They are cold eyes," I answered, " as the hands are cold when the blood that should warm them is overcharging the heart or head. When all the powers of being are strained to one vital point, the balance of character is lost. I make out this Lady of the Rock to have been no miracle of perfection, but simply a woman brave and passionate, proud and single, who will admit no profanation of her love. It is not in nature that a contest long and unequal and terrible

as this of hers, could be maintained without sacrifice,
or come out of without scars."·

"Ha, this hardness, it is as a scab upon her, you
would say," returned the Swiss.

"An' if it wass, the loss of her own true love must
have cut her deep enough whatever," said Miss Macorquodale.

"I find for all you may show that such sores look
ugly on a smooth skin," sneered the pedlar.

"The more's the pity!" retorted Miss Macorquodale; and I was satisfied to leave the last word with
her; it had gone to the heart of the matter.

"It is the highest tide that has been known in
these parts since I was a lad," said Mr. Cumming,
returning from the window at which he had been
listening with an ear which was of Arab fineness, to
the signs without. "The waves that were washing
up when I came in, are over the foot of the Castle
rock the now. The lady" (making a motion towards
me, for my secret was out) "has alluded in her poem
to the high spring-tide."

"And accident," said I, glancing at the pedlar, "is
lending itself to the effect of my 'decor.' We shall
have more to do with the tide as the poem proceeds.
It was just at this season, and at the close of just such
a day, that what you are going to hear came to pass."

"We have been stayed from it too long, if I may

make bold to say so," said our host, resuming his
contemplative attitude. But we were constrained to
wait a while longer, for Miss Macorquodale, who had
been plying old Susan with additional refreshment,
and pressing a raw egg upon the reader, was now
upon her knees beside the hearth, peering with a
face expressive of the liveliest concern into a chink
made by the raising of the inverted pot beneath
which our "first dinner" was baking. As all within
this aperture looked to me dark as Erebus, and as it
could hardly be that the savoury odour which was
diffusing itself in the kitchen could convey exact
information of the stage reached in the cooking, even
to the most experienced nostrils, I am at a loss to
divine by what occult process she arrived at the reassuring conclusion of which her countenance gave
evidence. However that may have been, the odour
was such as would have been found highly stimulat-
ing to the appetite in any other house than that over
which Miss Macorquodale presided, and might even
in some cases have created a diversion in the thoughts
of the audience, unfavourable to intellectual impres-
sions ; but for those who were subject to her motherly
ministration, material need was so completely anticipated, that not even the homeless wanderer was seen
to turn an eye in the direction of the seething viands.

When Miss Macorquodale resumed her place, she

did not again take up her knitting, but spreading her
apron over her hands in token that their service was
suspended for the present, composed her face to a
flattering show of interest.

FITTE THE FIFTH.

My lady sat in her bower, and span
   From a newly plenished creel ;
She loved the wild sea noise that drowned
   The droning of her wheel,
Nor feared to hear the low winds race
Through the tall spear-grass to their meeting-place.

But the restless wind awoke her heart
   Where her love was laid asleep,
And it rose up wild like a startled child,
   It waked like a child to weep ;—
O world forlorn in the wan grey weather,
And young heart weeping and wailing together !

For the wrestling wind recalled a time
   When the grey wan world was green,
When the sun was high, her lost love nigh,
   And the sting of love so keen

In the stroke that cleft her heart in twain,
She knew not if it were joy or pain.

The wind, the waves, the droning wheel,—
   No new sound thrilled the air,
But her flesh made motion that some strange thing,
   Some loathly to life, stood there.
She stopped her wheel, the fine thread broke ;
It was her lord, he laughed, he spoke :
" Would'st give your thought in my thought's
       stead,
You'd win by the exchange," he said.

She turned from him, she locked her hands
   And laid them athwart her breast ;
She feared belike his questing gaze
   From sanctuary might wrest
A name she knew the faintest breath
Betraying, would betray to death.

" Put by your wheel and spin no more,
   Come, lady, and come with me ;
You ever have loved the singing wind,
   You love the dancing sea ;
My biorlin is on the shore,
Leave flax and fancies, spin no more."

His voice was soft, his words were smooth,
　His eye had a feline glow,
You seemed to see it burn more bright
　That the light was waxing low.
He smiled, repeating as before :
" Leave flax and fancies, spin no more."

She left her wheel, she left her bower,
　She followed the false Maclean,
The piper piped them to the shore,
　He piped a doleful strain :
The pibroch of Macrimmon Môr :
" The way you go you'll come no more."

The chieftain's foster-brethren twain
　Hung on to the shallop's side,
That shook in the breeze as a courser shakes
　Ere he steadies himself in his stride ;
The lady barely brooked their help,
　In her strength of youth and pride ;
They back the boat through the blown sea-scurf
And board her all in the boiling surf.

The helm was ta'en of the red Maclean,
　The oars by Donald Dhu,
And Shamesh, he of the bloody hands—
　And they were a grisly crew ;

But my lady's spirit rose bold and free
'Twixt the singing wind and the dancing sea.

O youth, what art thou for gallant stuff?
  Well known to the fiend Despair,
Of him you haply will take of Death
  But never will doff to Care ;
A gleam of sun, a breath of brine,
Will mount your pulses as brisk new wine.

The good boat breasted the creaming waves,
  She rose in the teeth of the breeze,
She charged again as a fiery steed
  When stricken aback by the seas.
The mountains seemed to soar and dive ;
The dim world heaved as yet alive.

The Norse-built keep of Castle Duart,
  That one while, gaunt and bare,
Looked glowering from its stony height,
  Melted as smoke in air';
As faint from that dissolving shore
The pibroch wailed, " You'll come no more."

But where the two winds meet, the drift
  Had loosed a lurid cloud

Which floated up as the sun went down—
   In fashion as a shroud,
Or liker to a woman drowned,
With arms outspread, and hair unbound.

As the rowers caught in the lady's eyes
   A shadow of vague affright,
They turned about on their labouring oars,
   To question the waning light;
And deep in the downdraught of one thought
A moment those four souls were caught.

Then looked at her with wolfish eyes
   And fierce, the red Maclean;
Then looked at her with conscious eyes
   And keen, those gillies twain;
Their meeting glances quelled her breath,
They seemed to smite, and deal her death.

The pibroch's note was heard no more,
   The pallid mist had spread
O'er all the world a winding-sheet
   For all the world seemed dead;
The wind and the waves upon its track
Shrieking the lost world's coronach.

But broadening over their bows they see
   A line of angry foam

That hard on a bare, nigh-sunken rock
  With maddened haste beats home ;
And all the woe that was no more,
The dead world's woe, was in its roar.

The lady heard, and she rose up pale,
  In the quivering boat upright ;
It was but the blind young blood that rose,
  Alas ! what hope in flight,
What hope of any help might be
Betwixt the dead world and the sea ?

And looking ahead where the breakers struck
  The black, low-lying shore,
'Twas a man's hoarse voice that smote her ear—
  Smote through the deafening roar :
" There one in love with death," it said,
" Might have white sheets for a marriage-bed."

Then not for tumult of wind or wave
  That lady's heart beat high,
It swung with the dead, dull weight of lead,
  It struck as for danger nigh
A wild alarum, whereat each sense
Doubled the force of its frail defence.

And, served by the drift of the landward seas,
  The boat makes straight for the rock ;

She shoots the waves, and in the trough
  Lies stunned as if with the shock;
Then rights herself as fearing more
The helmsman than the deadly shore.

Dumb 'mid the thunder of wind and surge,
  That savage helmsman steers,
The world in lapsing from out their sight
  Is clamouring at their ears;
But through the tumult they can feel
The shingles grind a quivering keel.

And swept ashore on a towardly wave,
  They haul the good boat in,
And without a word the brethren fall
  To work in the wildering din:
Some deadlier task, and still to come,
Would seem to hold those brethren dumb.

Then swift as strokes of the stormy sea,
  More rude than the raging wind,
The lady is 'ware of two sudden arms
  That seize her body and bind,
And knows from its beating that dull way
The heart her dagger had kept at bay.

The red Maclean! none other than he,
  He has her in hand at last,

L

And oh, ye smouldering fires of hell!
   This time he holds her fast;
The teeth of the dragon beneath her vest
Are buried deep in her bleeding breast.

He stood with his bride on that trampled shore—
   They two, and they alone—
And with brackish kisses he pressed and pressed
   As one who would make his own
Her shuddering lips; then he cast her down
   As a man might cast a stone,
And the rock that was all that was left of the world
Seemed sinking with that light weight so hurled.

He turned where the tattered fringe of the sea
   Lighted the falling night;
That face, that face on the brown sea-ware
   Had shown so ghastly white!
He dares the foaming wrath of the surge,
   He boards his boat as in flight,
He shouts: "Haste, brothers, make for the large!"
The waves are roaring a countercharge.

The foster-brothers they heave their hearts
   Loud beating against the prow,
But in face of the countervailing sea
   The labour of man is slow;

And somewhat white hangs on to the boat,
Forbearing the shallop to get afloat:

Ah! what but the swift young blood again,
  Uprisen as with a cry—
The voice of its still-aspiring life
  "Not yet is it time to die,"
Has sent my lady in this wild way
With grappling hands to plead and to pray?

He struck her off, the caitiff Maclean—
  The very breakers had fled
To let her kneel—but there be lost men
  And damned or ere they be dead.
"Kneel, woman, kneel," said the red Maclean,
"And kneel as once I knelt—in vain!"

The sea in its sovereign strength returned
  And took the maid to its breast,
Then arched itself—a triumphant wave—
  And bore her high on its crest,
To lay the face so ghostly fair
Unharmed again on the brown sea-ware.

My lady rose in the strength of her pride,
  She saw herself there alone—

She rose and blest the sundering sea,
    The islet was all her own ;
She rose and rose to its topmost ledge—
    She made thereof a throne ;—
She cried : " Maclean of Duart, farewell !
We're parted now as heaven and hell ! "

No blot on the shrouding mist, Maclean
    With his whole dark world seemed dead,
All, even to very hate of him,
    Gone like a knotless thread,
So that behind, as about, above,
Was nothing left her but Death and Love.

Then she wept for ruth of her maiden truth :
    " O Love, have I waked for thee
By day and night, but to face thee now
    With this lothèd stain on me ?
Come, ocean, and with your bitter brine
Sweeten these ravished lips of mine ! "

The hydra heads of the western waves
    Broke, parted to north and south,
They lipped the shore, commixed, and closed
    As one vast, foaming mouth
That hungered for her evermore,
That all but slew her with its roar.

And still she called upon Love : " False Love,
   To think thy summery breath
Should drive a soul that trusted thee
   On this wild way of death ! "
The foam-fringed rock was wearing small,
Scarce bigger now than a maiden's pall.

The clamouring surges formed and fell,
   Pressed nearer and yet more near,
Then plunged and quivered in pale recoil
   Of pity, or eke of fear.
They broke, they wandered round her seat—
They went, they came, they licked her feet.

And still she cried and still she clung :
   " O treacherous sea, and slow,
Come take my life and make an end,
   Since death will have it so ! "
The mad sea melted at her commands,
Came back and kissed her clinging hands.

The charging waves come on, fall off,
   Rise, sheer as a wall, and steep—
O Christ, must the whole dead world go down,
   Entombed in the charnel deep?
The strong tide lays her bosom bare,
She feels it dragging her tangled hair.

Her hands have ceased to clasp and cling,
  She has shaken her spirit free,
She will strive no more, she will make no moan,
  She will go with the clamouring sea.
The waves ring only against the rock,
But it feels as yielding beneath the shock.

And still the breakers lift their crests,
  " O maiden Mary," she cries,
"Who will tell my lover my heart was true,
  Who will right me in love's eyes ? "
But the hydra heads have come and gone,
And in face of death she still lives on.

But they come no more, dear God, so nigh
  They come not again, they fall
And trample the rock beside her feet,
  Fierce monsters, but held in thrall,
Tamed in their very pride's excess
To this turbulent show of humbleness.

The battle-front of the daunted sea,
  Though the waves still chop and churn,
Is in forced retreat, the wavering tide
  Has trembled long on the turn ;
Then one white wave came back and surged
About her—and her lips were purged.

And she lay there washed as for the grave,
  And purer than virgin snow,
Her beauty seemed as a conquering power
  In this its overthrow ;
Her eyes were blinded, choked her breath,
Her ears were open gates of death.

A panic seized on the routed waves :
  They fled to the sandy shelves,
They writhed, they foamed, they broke, they
    turned,
  And foundered upon themselves ;
But in that maiden was no stir ;
Great Love had had his will of her.

The terror deepened upon the sea,
  The stillness grew on the wind ;
They fled together, these fierce allies,
  And left their spoil behind—
The one sole thing that glimmered white
And pure in all that world of night.

The reader looked round when his voice had
ceased ; but the audience whom his passionate sympathy had been helping to magnetise, was smaller
than when the last Fitte had begun by the defection

of our foreign friend. The tall old cuckoo clock in the corner, after giving its grumbling warning, had struck one with an air of such sudden decision, that the casual guest, who in a vague way had been getting to feel himself more and more out of harmony with his surroundings, caught the infection, and determined on the instant to push on for Tobermory. This resolution was more easily arrived at, in that with the turn of the tide there had come a lull in the storm ; and it was further reinforced by the reflection that if Tobermory was to be gained before nightfall, there was not a moment to lose. At about the middle of the last canto, therefore, and just in the seemingly blackest moment of the Lady of the Rock's impending doom, the hawker had hastily risen, had seized his full pack and his empty tray, had settled them in their places with a hitch of his shoulder, and pointing his knotted stick vaguely into the open with a gesture which the expression of his countenance made almost threatening, included us all in one valedictory nod, and addressed himself to his wandering way. As both Auchnacraig and Craigie-nure were within reasonable distance in the event of the return of the storm, and as it was supposed that one who knew so well the business of other people would not be wholly ignorant of his own, no motion was made to detain him ; and with the exception of an inarticulate protest on the part of Miss Macorquodale, and, as a recoil from the chilling effect of this departure, an effort at deeper abstraction on that of her nephew, the reading had proceeded without a break. I pass over the eager comments which greeted the finish of the last canto, for as they were all in different keys of sympathetic approval, they could possess no interest for any but ourselves.

"I reckon the gaberlunzie man would have bided to the end, had he found a better market for his creeticisms," remarked Archie Cumming, when reader and writer had been made sufficiently happy.

"The chentleman knew how to cheapen them," said old Susan, and the fun that found its way out of her eyes made them almost uncanny.

"His voice was as harsh as a rusty hinge," said Miss Macorquodale, "but the chentleman and the wind together were too many for him."

"I am glad at heart," remarked Cumming, "to have got hold of this spirited lady to stand up against the bad Maclean in place o' the feckless body that has been bearing with him too long."

"I'd be gladder still to know," exclaimed Miss Macorquodale, "that there wass some one on the other side to show her a warm fire, and gi'e her a dry change."

"The sun may happen look out after the storm,"

returned Mr. Cumming, "and sunshine is more comforting than fire, as hope, which the leddy had, is more cordial than wine."

"That's true," assented his aunt, "and there iss no man wi' a plaid, and no Scot iss without on sic a night, but would ha' wrapped it about her whatever."

"I ken the pibroch," quavered old Susan from out of the glow of just such a fire as her hostess had been invoking for the Lady of the Rock,—"I ken the pibroch, an' it be the ane that scared the wolves frae the piper in the cave sae lang's he had the breath to blow it."

"Ay, ay, we all ken it," said Miss Macorquodale; "they play it at the buryings, and most of us have heard it too often."

"We call it Macrimmon's Lament," said her nephew; "it has got a wail in it like the wail o' the wind, and yet I have heard it skirl as if for joy, as the wind too will do at whiles to my thinking."

The clock struck the quarter at this moment.

"Get along wi' ye, Maisie, and lay the things for the first parlour dinner," exclaimed Miss Macorquodale; but as at the reminder of the hour the few remaining pages of manuscript had been hastily resumed, the girl tossed the spoon she had been rubbing on to a tray, which she speedily covered with

a heterogeneous mass of plates and knives, of jugs,
and even of basins, and had just seized the whole
ill-assorted burthen to bear it away with her young
might, when her gentle-hearted mistress, attracted
by the unnecessary noise, looked up, and caught a
glance of such tearful and even pettish appeal, that
she rose with the apologetic remark :

"She's no but a lassie, and words iss to her almost
as much as things iss to those that know better ; " and
bidding Maisie put down the tray, and exercise her
prowess upon polishing a dish-cover, she made a
more thoughtful selection of the things whose value
had been so misprized, and departed on her volun-
tary exile.

From five the audience was now reduced to three ;
but poor as it was numerically, its quality was excellent. It was truly "fit" if "few." There was
the old woman, whose work in the world being done,
had no need and no desire to be elsewhere than she
was ; there was the man in whom sustained attention
had been trained to habit ; who could have sat or
stood out the longest sermon ; and there was the girl
with her unsated hunger for all that was wild and
wonderful, the yet untouched chords of her being,
ready to give back unquestioning answer to the voice
of old romance. These people judging me by the
heart and ear, liking or leaving for themselves, with

no sense of obligation to a higher court, no cowardly
or obsequious holding back, no pretended discovery
of merits which they had been bidden to feel,—this
was a rare chance, and one hardly to be looked for
nearer than the Island of Mull.

As the poem proceeded to its close, my own words
came back to me with a music which, though not
wholly mine, was felt more precious by the isolated
human soul for the unconscious collaborations.

FITTE THE SIXTH.

Two shapes passed over the sobbing sea
  To land at Dunolly Bay ;
One passed at sunrise, one at noon
  Of the new-created day.
The first was a work of God undone ;
The second, a devil's but ill begun.

And both were silent as outer space,
  Both white as the upper air ;
As one mask lay to the rising sun,
  And one to the noon-day bare,
Broke from the first a gasping breath,
Shone on the second the beads of death.

So the first was laid on the yellow sands
  To catch the coming of day,

And the second was covered up close as night
   To hide from the noon away ;
And light of life came into the first,
But the second sweltered, a thing accurst.

Through the standing floods, by the lonely
      ways,
   In the tracks which the sheep had worn,
By Shamesh, he of the bloody hands,
   That spotless lady is borne ;
But her sleeping sense of his care is fain,
And his bloody hands leave never a stain.

He had sighted her soul when it rose and sued
   To his chief at her wild wide eyes ;
And the sea and the shore through the live-
      long night
   Had been ringing as with her cries ;
And they drew him whether he would or no
With the cords of a man, and he had to go.

So he found her there where the sea had laid
   And left her, but not a sound
There breathed from her body, as mournfully
   The waves fell sobbing round ;
Then a stainless lily, alive or dead,
He gathered her up in his hands, and fled.

Then as bloody Shamesh was making the shore,
  And laying that white ladye
In the sun's warm bed on the yellow sands,
  Maclean was putting to sea
With the waxen shape that in hate of hell
His limmer had molten and made so well.

But or ever the seeming widower
  Had come with the seeming dead
To Dunolly Bay, that first true twain
  Were well on their journey sped,—
Ben Cruachan behind them, frowning above
And blocking the way of the foes of love.

Then they hail the ferry, and lightly go
  Where heavily erst she came,
And the jubilant song of Glenara fall
  Sets her frozen blood aflame,
And she lights at the gate, and she seems to win
Her way like a chartered ghost within.

And she glides to her place by the arras screen,
  And faces her kinsmen all,
For a wandering breath that told of her death
  Had called them together in hall :
"You must open your hearts as of yore to me,
For you get me back at the gift of the sea !"

They opened their hearts, and they lent their ears
  To her tale, but on every dirk
A hand was locked in a fast embrace
  And with promise of wilder work
Than ever had been in the age-long reign
Of hate 'twixt Clan Campbell and Clan Maclean.

Then the women swarmed round her and bore her
    away,
  As a leaf on a stream at flood,
They shrieked wild curses, but eased their hearts
  With tears, while they talked of blood ;
And my lady who heard was resolving it all
In the call of the cuckoo, the song of the fall.

But when, brave and sweet, from her maiden bower
  She issued again, they had done ;
And the whole clan rose to the queen of the
    feast,
  And she faced them, and saw but one,
Till her thought was drawn to that vanished shore
By the ghost of the dirge of Macrimmon Môr.

Faint as a travelling spirit of sound
  It came and went on the breeze,
Now low in the valley, now high on the hill,
  Now lost in the leaves of the trees ;

But ever emerging, and ever more near,
As the men clutched their dirks and bent forward
    to hear,
For they knew of the thing that was like to appear.

A lie will be loud in its own defence,
  As a fearsome heart will be bold ;
And in every clachan the thing went through,
  The lie had been told and told,
And the dool of the lady lamented o'er
In the wild death-song of Macrimmon Môr.

Now it wails, it shrieks, it is passing the cross,
  It has entered the gate, and the beat
Grows loud and louder, the steady ground-tone
  Of an army of tramping feet ;
Then the great hall fills with a funeral train,
And in weeds of mourning the false Maclean

Steps warily close to an open bier,
  With one downward fiery eye
That has found a way through his folded plaid
  Fast fixed on the waxen lie ;
Then he lifts his hand and he stops the march
Of the train in the favouring gloom of an arch.

And one clan halts in the cavernous shade,
  One stands in a bright half ring

By the torch-lit board, each man in his place,
  But alert, and ready to spring
If damnable treason for once overbore
The bloodless craft of MacCallum Môr.

Then from out of the darkness a hollow voice
  Comes deep as the gloom and dull,
And the Campbells are fretting like hounds in leash,
  While the tortuous lord of Mull
Pours the tale of his loss and his dole in their ears
While his false eyes verily shed false tears.

"Abide, my brothers!" MacCallum Môr
  Has taken his sister's hand,
And adown the hall in their Campbell pride
  They pace together, and stand
In a halo of light by the open bier,
  He waving a burning brand
In the false dead face which wears flat in the flare,
As the falser living shrinks back from the glare.

But the lady has fronted the men of Argyle,
  And though never a sign gave she,
Her heart on another's made silent call,
  And the twain were suddenly three,
· She holding in ward with her maiden might
The armed right hand of her own true knight.

                                        M

The mourner has turned in his ghastly rear
  From that deadlier image than death,—
And lo, on the topmost stair, as of life,
  Sees the Lady Elizabeth,
And the radiant vision had all but slain,
As with effluent being, that caitiff Maclean.

His lieges are thronging in hall and court,
  And many bold men and true,
But in view of that lady who dazzles their eyes
  They cower and tremble too :
'Tis an unkenned sight, and a weird, to see
A spirit stand clear of its own bodie.

Now Maclean lies bleeding and overthrown
  In his recreant haste to fly ;
But MacCallum Môr had foreseen his gain
  In the life of his false ally,
Though his fiercer namesmen had all but broke
From his cautious hold, when his sister spoke.

She spoke in her tolerant scorn : "This chief
  Has suffered some wrong of me,
Which failing to right, he went near to avenge
  In the strength of his fere the Sea.
I stand here victor : let no man dare
To take from the vanquished the life I spare !"

She seized the brand, and tossed it alive
  On the waxen shape where it lay,
And the light full-fed leaped up to the roof,
  And the night was a brighter day.
Then the red Maclean, who, dabbled with gore,
And abject with terror, fled out of the door,
To his whilom lady became no more.

And she spoke again to her own true love,
  None hearing but only he :
" Forgive that a traitor in love's despite
  Once dared in sight of the sea—
But only once—high God He knows—
  To touch the lips of me,
Sith the great white wave that broke from above
Hath made them meet now for death or for love."

Then she turned in her pride to her feudal lord,
  Said, " Brother, now give me shrift ;
I was offered to shame, I was offered to death ;
  As I hold at the sea's free gift
My life and love, I will hold them fast,
Or find me a grave with the true at last."

But her brother has taken and joined their hands,
  And so soothfast was the kiss—

So dear love's due to her lips so true—
  She had like to have died of bliss;
Then over her cheek as she drooped her head,
Love's banner at last rose red, rose red.

  "There's an end of the Rhyme of the Lady of the Rock," said Helmuth.

  For a minute or two there reigned a silence in the kitchen, broken only by the occasional sound of water boiling over from a pot, and the soft lapping of the wood flames. Mr. Cumming had thrust his two hands deep down into the pockets of his coat, and was looking up at the smoke-stained rafters, as one who, having knowledge of the several roads from dreamland, has the taste to choose the longest. Highland Maisie was also looking out upon space from which the phantoms had not yet departed, her brown eyes at full stretch, while her hands were still mechanically engaged on their work of friction. Likely enough she was vivifying, if half unconciously, the ideal with a touch of the real.   Into this pause broke the heavily-shod tread of Miss Macorquodale, whose work of laying the cloth, making up the fire, and general straightening, was over in the parlour; and at this sudden irruption of the actual, the dish-cover fell from Maisie's hand to the floor, and in the shallow clatter of the tin, the final echo of the spell we had been seeking to prolong was dissolved. A cry of despair from the hearth, over which Miss Macorquodale had immediately doubled herself, completed the disenchantment.

"The potatoes iss boiled to just one smash," said Miss Macorquodale; "they will be no but good for the pigs."

We at once declared ourselves equal to doing without them, and professed our willingness even that the pigs should profit by the ill chance; for all which our provider bestirred herself to drain off the water, and to spread over the fractured vegetables a white cloth which she covered in closely with the lid of the pot, while, assisted by the conscience-stricken Maisie, she proceeded to disinter from its surrounding ashes the vessel which was serving as an oven, and to extricate its now perfectly cooked contents.

While this last dexterous feat was still in progress, we, feeling that the time was come for us to withdraw, approached the hearth in order to take leave of old Susan. It was then we discovered that the small audience of which I at least had been so fain—— the audience of three simple souls—had still further diminished during the last canto. The old woman on her cosy chair, in front of the comforting blaze whose babbling tongues had accompanied the mellow

reading voice, had succumbed to the combined influence, and was—oh, where it is so good to be,
where in her case we could almost have wished
she might ever have been suffered to remain—
asleep.

Our kind Miss Macorquodale looked at me. For
all her material solicitude, she was fully capable of
feeling for the artist in the defection of the one whom
she probably regarded as the most capable of the
assembled judges.

" Now who wass to know that the drop o' whisky
just put into her milk would ha' done that ? " she
asked, endeavouring to protect us both with the
ample shield of her benevolence.

" We will not wake her," I said, looking upon the
aged pilgrim whom life and time had robbed and left
so destitute ; "my verses have perhaps done the truest
service that they are ever destined to accomplish."

" I thank you kindly, sir," said Mr. Cumming,
looking Helmuth full in the face with his fervent
dreamy eyes as we passed him on our way to the parlour. To me he said not a word, but he bent his
small, well-set head, furnished with the high dome
which betrayed the ready enthusiast, and I knew
that he thought the thing that I had done was worth
the doing.

Crossing our steps before we reached the door, and

passing out through the entry with a motion almost
as rapid as that of a hare in flight, we encountered
the bent figure of Maisie. I felt her touch my hand
as she went with something that was other than her
own ; she was gone before I could receive the object
into my grasp, but on the ground I perceived, picked
up, and shall for ever cherish, a sprig of white heather
which I knew to be charged with her thanks and
praises. The girl was so overwhelmed with the sense
of her own boldness, that she was unable to appear
for the rest of the day, and the task of attending us
devolved wholly on Miss Macorquodale.

The pedant had gone his ways, not knowing and
not caring for the end, condemning the whole from
what it pleased him to regard as the imperfection of
a part, accounting of the work but as a text for the
display of his superior knowledge. The kindly,
serviceable woman who had us all in keeping, had
also risen before the close in answer to her own
proper call. For the weary wayfarer on a path
which had grown so desolate, my verses had anticipated the coming rest. It was all in order, all as it
should be, for I had had my moment of joy when
on the window-seat in the old Castle the thoughts
were seething within me ; and yet a vocation upon
which you have entered with the spirit of a votary
means the sacrifice, the dedication at least, of your

best energies to a single end,—the forsaking of all other objects and cleaving wholly to that one,—and where the inward impulse lacks the outward seal of success, the faith in such a call must inevitably be wavering; there will be moments of unutterable discouragement when the singer, hearing no answer to his own voice, will feel that the powers of which he is conscious could have been used, if directed more wisely, to better result for himself and for his kind. But the impulse to plough, not the fields of earth, but the air, has been obeyed, and however unyielding it has proved, it were fatal to fall back. It may be hoped that the Lord of all harvests will not deem the work to which He has been thought to summon, to have merited rebuke. In the meantime I was glad that a simple-hearted enthusiast was still to be found in a forgotten corner of the earth, and rejoiced with a greater singer in the reflection that the half of the human race at any given time and place is always under twenty years of age.

THE END.

PRINTED BY BALLANTYNE, HANSON AND CO.
EDINBURGH AND LONDON.